This book is dedicated to

Rebecca, Tiger and Frances

Conversations with Jim Morrison and Other Rock Legends

Featuring Michael Hutchence, Kurt Cobain,
Jimi Hendrix and Sid Vicious

Jacqueline Murray

Foreword

Jacqueline Murray first contacted me in 2005 to request a reading. This was just before she realized that she was also a gifted medium, and she had no idea what a truly gifted medium she was about to become. In our first reading, she specifically asked me to bring in her two friends Jim and Michael, who had both passed away tragically. I brought them both forward as they were eager to speak. I described their personalities and circumstances surrounding their deaths as each of them were shown to me. I actually had no idea at first who they really were in their earth lives.

Jim came into the first reading as a tortured artist type. He said he was a writer and poet. I felt such sadness about him but I also sensed an aggressive and impatient nature. It wasn't long before he had me tell Jacquie that he wanted to write a book with her. She said she was honored but I could see how confused she was. She really didn't know what to make of it, and I'm sure at the time she really didn't take the statement all that seriously.

Michael Hutchence also came in as a tortured soul. He was very sad and rather quiet at that first reading. He showed me vague flashes of his suicide and told me how he regretted it as soon as it happened. He insisted it was not premeditated. Then I saw his daughter, and I was overwhelmed by his depression. He has made great strides since then with his ascension and so has Jim. I don't recognize either of their vibrations today as they were just a few years ago.

By the third reading, Jacquie told me she didn't actually know Jim Morrison or Michael Hutchence personally. Ordinarily, I might have raised an eyebrow and concluded she was an obsessed fan, but I knew these spirits actually wanted to be around her as if they did know her personally. Jacquie told me that they simply showed up one day. She wasn't sure what was going on, but she certainly needed confirmation, so she contacted to a few mediums. Not being a formally trained medium or even having an interest, it's no wonder she considered checking into the nearest nut hut. Fortunately, she chose to investigate other possibilities first. Choosing a psychiatric evaluation probably would have shut the doors to the truth as I feel they have for many people who unknowingly channel spirits from the other side. Private readings with me and other people confirmed Jacqueline Murray to be quite sane in fact.

It is understandable that Jacquie continued her doubts as a channel for quite some time. Never-the-less, she took pen to paper and wrote down every word that was given to her. Readings with me and others would eventually take on new purpose. Jacquie no longer needed to validate herself as a medium after a while, but as the channeled material piled up—notebook after notebook—she would often seek to validate certain content and make sure she was hearing things correctly. For two years she channeled her first book with Jim and Michael. *A Tale of Two Brothers: Jim Morrison and Michael Hutchence* was published in March of 2008 through authorhouse.com. Jim and Michael both speak the truth about their sad, early crossings, offer some personal messages to those who knew them and speak about life on the other side. They also give insights into our humanity. *A Tale of Two Brothers* has been endorsed by several reputable and well-known psychics and mediums, and some—including myself—have contributed sections. No sooner did the book become available to the public and radio interviews were being scheduled, Jacquie was told by Jim Morrison that it was time for more. She knew there were others Jim had lined up waiting to spcak with hcr, but she had very little free time beyond cordial greetings while channeling the first book. It seemed that Jim especially wanted this second book to introduce other musicians and friends. All I can say is that this channel has certainly been a good sport.

Jacqueline Murray has been very gracious to channel these spirits. She has not asked for anything from them in return. She never asked to be a medium and actually had no interested. She told me that was never even a fan. She has however accepted that Jim and Michael have chosen her as their exclusive channel.

It is my hope that you'll enjoy *Conversations with Jim Morrison and Other Rock Legends* as much as I have. You'll feel like Jim Morrison is your host in this book. After several hundred pages of the first book, he and his co-host Michael Hutchence, both still have much to say from the other side, and this time they brought friends. They'll introduce conversations with Kurt Cobain, Jimi Hendrix and Sid Vicious and others. Fans will also enjoy several new lyrics channeled within these pages. Whether you are a rock fan from years gone by or simply interested in raising your vibrations, there are personal messages for some and deep insights for us all in the pages ahead.

Conversations with Jim Morrison and Other Rock Legends

© *Copyright 2009 Francine Milano*

All rights reserved. No part of this book may be used or reproduced in any form without prior written consent of Francine Milano (www.francinemilano.com) with exception to brief, quoted excerpts embodied in articles or reviews.

Visit www.booksurge.com to order additional copies.

ISBN: 1-4392-2275-4

Printed in the United States

Contents

	Foreword	v
Introduction		1
Chapter 1	Shaman's Blues	5
Chapter 2	The Provocateurs	33
Chapter 3	Heavenly Brilliance	73
Chapter 4	Walk with Me and Find Your Truth	111
Chapter 5	A New Dimension	121
Chapter 6	Poet's Lament	131
Chapter 7	The Dark Stars	149

Introduction

Jac = Jacqueline Murray (Channel)
Jim = Jim Morrison

Jac: Hello again Jim, I am surprised you have returned to channel some more.

Jim: Well this time, it's going to be like a big party, as some of my friends from this side will be joining us. And I have some things to say to you Jacquie.

Jac: Alrightee, go ahead.

Jim: I was not at all pleased with the editing of our first book together ("A TALE OF TWO BROTHERS, JIM MORRISON & MICHAEL HUTCHENCE"). Hundreds of pages were taken out.

Jac: I realize that Jim but I had to trust the editor because it was over 1,100 pages, and your channeling was going all over the place.

Jim: Jacquie, you were chosen for this because you would not edit our words or censor our thoughts out of a sense of righteousness or what you may call, political correctness. I am not "PC" Jacquie. I never was and even on this side, I never will be. We are here to give you our exact words and we ask that you take them down precisely as we give them to you, no editing this time, no changes, ok?

Jac: But Jim, I always go back and think about the fact, there are people on earth today who knew you and you meant something to them. I never believed in any of this stuff years ago, so I want to take into consideration the feelings of others.

Jim: That's sweet, but I suggest, we let the reader decide. The reader may view this as good, great, bad, awful, offensive, inane, bizarre or many other things. Our one hope is, it makes them think about what they think they know, versus the actual truth which is rarely in print these days. Your desire to mask some of the truth in the name of not offending anyone must be removed if we are to continue. What is your concern? That someone is trying to protect my legacy (Laughs)?

Jac: Yes, your legacy and, also you had personal relationships with a variety of people. I am sure they want to defend you.

Jim: Defend me or profit from me? Make no mistake; those who have financially gained from my image have left a bad taste in my mouth in the past. I don't bother with such things now. How many more books or articles will be written and sold about me?

Jac: Well what are we doing here Jim?

Jim: We are not recycling the same old material. My so-called legacy ended in 1971. There is nothing new but for wasteful investigations into my death which never should've been covered up. My legacy is now so far removed from who I was and what I was trying to do, it's almost shameful people continue to harvest these writings and sell them to the public. This is new material Miss. These are things that no one has written about because they have no idea what really happened to me after I left the earth. You, like a good journalist, are getting the story.

Jac: But I'm not a journalist Jim or even a writer. I have never wanted to write a book.

Jim: You weren't aware you have this gift, Jacquie.

Jac: True.

Jim: I will be addressing the skeptics and critics this time and I don't want you to consider censoring my words. I am not concerned with how a reader takes this work, it is their free will. However, when they use my name and say this could not be me, it is insulting. I use to read my reviews on earth and take them quite personally. I held onto them. I think some of that is carrying over into this.

Jac: Not good Jim, seriously, I am sure many people have a really hard time believing this, as I did for a few years.

Jim: You can't learn anything new with a closed mind. Let's prepare to work. I wish someone I knew on earth named Sandra would visit Dr. Linda Salvin in L.A.

Jac: May I ask why Jim?

Jim: To get her head out of her ass

Jac: What?

Jim: Don't question me honey, just take it all down and let the chips fall where they may.

CHAPTER 1

Shaman's Blues

"The tears of the world are a constant quantity. For each one who begins to weep somewhere else another stops. The same is true of the laugh. Let us not then speak ill of our generation, it is not any unhappier than its predecessors. Let us not speak well of it either. Let us not speak of it at all. It is true the population has increased."

—*Samuel Beckett, Waiting for Godot*

Channel's Note: These are the words of the spirit who was known on earth as James Douglas Morrison (lead singer of the Doors). These are the words he gave me and you the reader, need to make-up your own mind.

Jim Morrison:

There are those who believe - and those who don't that this is me, the Jim Morrison you once knew (or thought you knew) speaking from the other side. Perhaps the non-believers should spend some time engrossed in Plato's "analogy of the divided line" as it will shed some much needed light on what is taking place here. I certainly had a discussion on earth about the "analogy of the divided line" but now am disdainful about that human exchange as I realize my own hypothesis of it was rather rigid, more so than I realized.

To understand who I was during that lifetime, I would refer to something else I discussed while a guest of Mother Earth, Plato's "allegory of the cave" and it certainly goes hand-in-hand with a quote attributed to me "Whoever controls the media, controls the mind." At a point in that short, blur of an existence, I was able to stand-up in the cave and go outside. Unfortunately, I remained disoriented until the day I left the grand hotel, the masterful mirage. I believe anyone who knew me on earth can simply refer to Plato's "allegory of the cave" and the "Four

Idols" presented by Sir Francis Bacon and realize, they represent the knowledge I possessed but it became twisted and at times indecipherable in its' delivery.

As I now look back at Plato (who inspired so many of the philosophers I came to relish), perhaps the least thing I understood was his "metaphor of the sun" and now, I can proclaim with great joy, nothing makes more sense to me.

As I think of what would've been on earth if I had survived that dreadful summer, I know I would've written a book of a somewhat similar nature to "*The Power of Myth*" by Joseph Campbell. I would not by any means have been able to capture its brilliance. But my mind was working in such a way, already by 1971, that this is precisely the type of book, I would've liked to have written in addition to a novel, (hell bent on destroying all that a novel should not be). A close male friend, who knew me better than most, read "*The Power of Myth*" and thought of me—as he does often.

I admire Joseph Campbell for his enigmatic presentation. Joseph was also inspired as I was, by a James Joyce book called "*Finnegan's Wake*" and I believe the illustrations in "*The Power of Myth*" (drawings and pictures), are equally as powerful as the words. "*The Power of Myth*" is a symphony for the subconscious even more so than the conscious mind.

I believe if even in a very small sense, you felt aware of me on earth, you will understand, the things I have just mentioned (if you bother to read and study them), are things I understood and at certain times, I tried to maneuver in a manner to fully grasp them. I was precocious in this comprehension of reality and in some ways, this continually set me apart.

Whether you are a believer, a non-believer or curiosity seeker, we can begin the ride. You have come here for your own reasons, and so have I.

There are messages I wish to give to a few of those who knew me on earth. Some of us will meet again, and in that space, most of you will get an apology that is both necessary and sincere. I could've been a better person to many of you but I often enjoyed being who you wanted me to be. It wasn't so much that I was a chameleon, more of a changeling (a child surreptitiously or unintentionally substituted for another). I went from being one emotionally immature man to another, purely for the benefit of the audience or the person around me.

I know someone who knew me not only wrote a song inspired by "Waiting for Godot" but feels in some strange way, that play is akin to me and he is not the only one I knew on earth who thinks that. I have a few earth friends who have memories or thoughts of me in relation to Samuel Beckett's timeless work. It's been publicly proclaimed that Beckett wrote it as a form of relaxation to take him away from the prose he has been composing at the time. That is how I composed a good deal of the time, in the whole stream of consciousness thing so it was not forced or contrived. "Waiting for Godot" seems in some ways, to be about some of the issues I dealt with while on earth and, it's the pathos of the work that I love, along with the use of language.

Beckett has often told of the paintings that inspired his great work, a painting known as "Man and Woman Contemplating the Moon" by Casper David Friedrich. Though Beckett sometimes referenced another painting featuring the moon, I want to talk about the man and woman painting. The painting captivates me and I understand why someone would be so enthralled with it. I think of my true eternal soul mate when I view this, and the two of us gazing at the moon as we will be, someday soon.

I really am rather occupied in my ethereal prison on this side. I am not one to check on or be all too concerned with those I left behind because when I saw my life unfold, the fast blur of deception and incarceration; I needed to retreat from all things of earth, minus my true eternal soul mate.

Looking back on wasted time, a wasted life and space will not do any of us any good. I only live now for my woman, and our life, which cannot come soon enough for me. I don't live in the past, or really long to see any of it.

A woman I once knew on earth has read this book called "Soul Mates" by a man named Thomas Moore. It's a good book with much to offer, especially to those who are going through life as I did, unfulfilled in terms of a romantic partnership. The woman who has been reading it, has been thinking for some time, that I am her true mate when she returns home and I am bringing this up, only to inform her, it's not so honey. I don't want her or anyone to believe they are the one I speak of from this side, as my true soul mate has already received a massive sign and validation of who she is and it's important that those who knew me on earth, or those fans of mine who think they could be her, to realize, she already knows, she has received something physically, that has no explanation and she has become aware. You have not received this sign from me, and while you may wish this to be true, and you may want to be my other half, hopefully you will let go of the delusion and perhaps you have someone waiting for you on earth or on this side.

I do not hold onto anyone I knew on earth. I am Godot, in essence, I will never show-up, at least not for them. You are waiting for something that will never be, because I have only one to share eternity with. I am not your fantasy. I am not your eternal soul lover. I am for her and she is for me. No one I knew on earth can change this because I was simply moving through life in stereo, looking, searching, but never finding. Alcohol was more important to me than any one woman, any song, any poem, any dream because she is my dream and I could not find her. I had to be numb. You try to hold onto me with your memories. How can you? Why would you choose to?

You cannot hold onto someone who has left you and will not return. It's fruitless. I am gone for good, and you may get an apology from me for not being what I could've been to you. But what you had on earth - is all there is. My life must evolve, and you, should let go.

I am nonplussed at some who try to be the "expert" on all things pertaining to Jim Morrison. I am not speaking of the other members of "The Doors." We were public figures together and I have no animosity with what they do, and owe each of them, an apology for not holding up my end.

To the others who speak of me frequently, excuse me, what gives you the right? Because you knew me, or thought you did? If you knew me so well, I would be interested to know why you didn't show-up in Paris and attempt to save my life in that fateful summer? I would wonder why you believe only having bits and pieces of me, in conversations we had makes you qualified to be an expert on me, especially considering I kept so much inside? I can tell you this, if you believed you "knew" me, you need to keep it in context. You don't "know" me anymore because I have evolved and I can see it all with great clarity. To believe I would be the same on this side would pretty much be putting me in a box, like I was thrown into during July, of 1971. I am not in that box, and you can't keep me in one. I know the freedom you can't begin to imagine.

If you believe you "knew" me, and I was so "special" to you, then perhaps it would be only fitting that you kept your thoughts of me, your precious memories to yourself. When someone is really special or meaningful in your life, it's best kept inside. You don't have to broadcast it to the universe and beyond. The world doesn't need to know; only you do. It's called having a sense of decorum or respect for someone you feel is worthy of those concepts. Do I deserve that from any of you? It seems not. This notion of saying "I knew Jim Morrison, and you didn't" is astounding. You say it with such petulance. Do you realize how insignificant and utterly absurd this is when you leave your body for eternity? Or how about this, let's decide this woman can't possibly be channeling the real Jim Morrison because he's not the Jim you knew (Laughs). Who was the Jim you "knew?" Or better yet, who did you "think" he was? You seem to know as little about my life as you do my death. The whole thing of, the mysterious death no one is sure about, demonstrates how much you know about my life. It's all conjecture based on the conjecture of others. I have been gone since 1971, do you think it may be time to let me go? I ask this only for your own good. I really don't like to see souls so stuck on earth as I was and I would not wish for anyone to be "stuck" over me or some faded memories of a man they hardly knew, could not hold onto and will not be with sometime in their future. Let's move on, because it was up to me to put the puzzle of my life together, not you.

"This is the strangest life I've ever known."

> —*Jim Morrison: "Waiting for the Sun" on the album Morrison Hotel (1970)*

Channel's Note: This material was channeled from the late, great Jim Morrison, formerly of The Door's in the spring of 2008. I have taken this down exactly as Jim has given it to me.

Jim Morrison:

I have told the official story of my life and death in the book "A Tale of Two Brothers: Jim Morrison & Michael Hutchence." I have given a naked version of what my life was about, the insanity of my alcoholism and the events surrounding my untimely death.

In this book, I want to talk about my adventures in the afterlife. Some have written some pretty fantastic fiction about my encounters on this side and some have written some pretty fantastic fiction they call biographies of my life. Not sure how you could write a biography of a person that never revealed himself fully to anyone and with so many of the pieces of the puzzle missing. I have given you those missing pieces in the first book I did through this channel. I will now complete the story by revealing my impressions of this side, revealing who I communicate with, and what I have learned.

It's funny that someone put me and Doc Holliday together in a story and claimed we are in hell, but that's not so inaccurate. I am in a sort of hell in this so-called heaven, but I did it to myself. I warn those reading this to fully comprehend my story, the mistake I made in leaving earth when I did. I have paid dearly since July the 3rd, 1971 A.D. I'm still paying.

Down, wanton, down! Have you no shame
That at the whisper of Love's name,
Or Beauty's, presto! up you raise
Your angry head and stand at gaze?

> —*Robert Graves (1895–1985), British poet, novelist. Down, Wanton, Down! Collected Poems (1965).*

Wanton Obsession

Channeled from Jim Morrison

I walked through your rose garden,
but saw nothing but daisies,
Where are your roses sweet woman?
Where do they hide?

I sat on your balcony,
stared at the moon,
Where are all your stars sweet woman?
Where do they hide?

I wrote you a song,
and sang it to you while you were dreaming,
I know it was not me you were seeing,
Who was it baby?

I wrote you a letter,
poured my heart out on my sleeve,
I stamped it and sent it,
Why have you not answered baby?

I come to you now,
deep in the night,
you have no dreams of me,
you have not replied to my letter
of angst - my open sores revealing
my unmitigated lust...
I won't go away until
you dream of me, until

you speak to me deep in
the night of what it is
you will do to me, as I give
you everything I am in
the most lascivious ways
I have ever expressed.

You have shaken my soul,
stirred my forensically analyzed
libido, I have no place to sleep
unless it's beside you my sweet
woman, dream of me, speak to me,
see me, only me.....

"Every church is a stone on the grave of a god-man: it does not want him to rise up again under any circumstances. "

—*Friedrich Nietzsche*

Testament of my great demise
(the lizard king bows out)

Channeled from Jim Morrison

Calling on the Gods,
Calling on the Gods,
why don't you answer me?

I've sacrificed as a rite of passage
I've done what I needed to do
in your name but nothing
has changed - Is it because
I've refused to change?

I drown myself in a bottle,
or two or three,
so I am loud,
obnoxious, coherent,
and incoherent,
capable and incapable,
drunk as a skunk,

so what is there of me?

What's left of me?
Do you hear me Apollo?
Do you see yourself
in me Dionysus?

Are you not of the trees?
Then why do you not
acknowledge me?

I look to the immortals,
as I am empty, I now call
on the Gods, wear an amulet,
study my totem, but only
my actions will transcend
my abysmal and
ferocious labyrinth

The demons of
the four winds have
clung to the bowels of
my soul, the magic
runes I possess may
abort them and absorb
their venom if I and

I alone cause this to happen
I no longer have a thirst to cleanse
my soul here on earth,

ZEUS, I know you hear
me with the beautiful Athena
Circe, answer me,
will you turn me
into swine? Can I stay
with you for a year?

Gaia, I must leave you now
for I have detached
myself from all people
and things that occupy your
once fertile landscape

I wish to return
to the hall of the immortals,
to the hall of the King
of Phaiakians,
as I seek the counsel
of Calchas and Orpheus

I wish to drink
from their golden chalices which
hold the fire of creation,
gaze deep into the ruby
flames where Gaia
herself can be recreated

Shekinah is calling me
now, softly, ever so softly,
but nonetheless she is
calling me home

I put down this pen,
and close my eyes now
for the last time....

You'll say I died
hugging the porcelain
of a toilet; you'll say

I succumb in a bathtub
from a derivative of
morphine as you try
to mask my desire
to join the immortals
and be reborn; as a Shaman

I wish to become like
Abaris and become a
Priest of Apollo, and
like the ancient Shaman,
become invisible and
foretell the future

I now know I have not done
what the Gods have
asked me to do

I have not driven
my own golden chariot
through the cosmos:

I need to start anew
I will just close my eyes.....
I only closed my eyes

Jim Morrison continues:

When I was around 22 or 23, I thought of dying young in an exciting way. Maybe a fiery crash like James Dean; I wanted something dramatic, colossal and talked about in the form of a legend for years to come. I wanted the manner in which I went out to be the stuff myths were made of. Once I got to the year 1969 and faced my fate due to the charges in Miami, I took a different view. It's true, I mellowed with age, and I became hopeful in the darkest nights and deepest depressions that maybe I could cultivate this beautiful, creative life anointed with the Gods of writing who would come to bless me and magically work through me.

By 1970, I was not interested in becoming a legend due to an abrupt and traumatic death. I began to hope for an easy death one day, no matter how it happened, I wished to just walk over to the other side in a calm and gentle sort of way. My great demise, so often discussed and debated with little fact behind any of it, did not occur that way. It was anything but easy and as far away from pleasant as anything I had ever known. I suffered, I was in pain, I was cold, and the five grueling hours felt like days. When it was over, I didn't just walk over, I was in silence and darkness and I am thankful that didn't last long. My soul exited my human body, coming through the top of my head. It's called the crown chakra. This may be a foreign concept to you and I never realized it happened this way, but this is how you leave your human body and that part is not only painless, it alleviates any sort of human suffering you may be in.

I was already gone when my body was being dragged across the Parisian apartment and placed, quiet stupidly in a bath tub. I did not want to return to that wretched, worn out body and I didn't want to return to that wretched, worn out existence. It was amazing to be out of body and it still is. It was the greatest trip I've ever taken and I didn't watch from above and think I wanted to go back to anyone or anything, because my great love was not present in Paris dragging me into a bath tub, she was in fact a little girl; this baby, who was unaware that her true eternal soul mate had just checked out, without waiting for her as he was suppose to. He checked out without as much as knowing of her existence but when I found out about her, all hell broke loose in my new home, the dimension most of you refer to as, heaven.

I had a difficult time coming to terms with the life I led as Jim Morrison, so difficult; I wish to God I had never been born into that abominable incarnation. I actually returned to Paris approximately two months later, in early September because I was heavily encouraged to figure out precisely or at least to some degree, what had gone wrong in the supposed city of my rebirth. (Why couldn't I start anew in Paris and close some of the doors in my life that were serving as demons and thieves of my youth, to open fresh ones and continue on?) I had this work I had set forth to do on earth even before James Douglas Morrison was born. I was to lead my flock so to speak to a new spirituality, a new birth and I came to earth to show others how to conquer to overthrow their dictators (personal demons). I would've mightily overthrown my dictators during my reign as a spiritual guru of a new and exciting renaissance about to take place in my private world of chaos.

I was given the staff and sword with my early fame that could've been transformed into a lasting presence of followers. I had inherited the throne by birth because it was the life path I had chosen before I came to earth as the man known as Jim Morrison. The lizard king was going to grow-up and evolve. He was going to become more spiritual and by doing so, his writing would've become deeper and deeper. I would've taken my followers along for the ride, provided they were willing to go; provided they were ready to go.

It's been suggested many times over; I died from a glorious drug trip, in a bath tub, or in a stall of the men's room in a Parisian nightclub. I can tell you this, I would've have absolutely preferred to have gone either of those ways as opposed to how I actually met the grim reaper. It was the most dreadful experience and a death I would not wish or want for anyone. If given the choice however, I would've never gone at twenty-seven and a half years of age. My life's purpose was left completely unfulfilled and most of all, I left behind my eternal soul mate, or as many would call her, my twin flame. It wasn't suppose to happen like that and due to what I did, in wearing out my body, in wearing down my body, in being around people who were not anymore coherent or able to help me than I was capable of helping myself; I have lived with this burden of enormous regret. I have been in such pain, my soul in such turmoil, and the agony of it all, and this unending anger is beyond what I can describe to you.

I want to say, those who have wept for me, and my premature death should not have done so. I was happy to be freed from that tattered and torn body and that unfulfilled existence. I didn't wish to return to my body when I saw it from above. The part that certainly could warrant many tears is how I left the earth without connecting to the soul I came to connect to.

You will hear or have heard we all have many soul mates and while that is true, many of them are just lessons we must learn. But this part is not true for everyone, I was created as a co-dependent soul and this is why as Jim Morrison I was in fact, a loner that no one could penetrate on a deep or lasting level. She was not present on earth with me, she was the one and only one who could penetrate me on any and all conceivable levels, including levels I was unaware existed. I am happy to tell many of you, not all of you were created as I was. I think it's better not to be made this way because things happen - horrible things and you get separated from that soul you are dependent upon and made for, and it's hard to suggest there's a greater pain.

Some of us are created in this condition of having this twin flame and some are not. I am not saying God makes mistakes or that one soul in one situation is superior to another, but I can talk of my own complicated labyrinth that I have walked through since the third of July, 1971 A.D. and tell you, leaving your other half behind brings no peace, and at times, instills hostility, anger and shades of insanity even for a soul on this side. To watch her on earth, having holidays without you, or getting her feelings hurt and crying alone, when you hear her but cannot hold her has been more difficult than anything ever was while I was occupying a human body.

When I first got over to this side, I returned to Paris and not to my grotesque grave with the graffiti and dupes around it, but to the Place Des Vosges where I sat in front of the fountain as I had done on earth; this time I was contemplating how I allowed this grand interruption into my plans as Jim Morrison to occur. A little girl approached me holding a daisy and she handed it to me. I was not sure who this beautiful little blonde angel was but I smiled at her and accepted it. This sweet girl turned out to be Rebecca, my other half, and in her dream state as a child, she was able to briefly visit me. I was not aware who she was at that time but when I learned shortly thereafter of her identity, I became isolated on this side and angry. Her soul recognized my soul on a very deep, subconscious level. She knew her eternal soul mate had gone home way too early, and she gave me that daisy to say, she forgave me for leaving her. But how could she forgive me? I cannot yet forgive myself.

Heaven and Hell
Channeled from Jim Morrison

Where is heaven?
How can it be,
earth is so far away
from the stars?

Heaven isn't a place,
it's not the final destination.

You hold heaven in your heart,
because heaven is true love-
and I found it, I found her
and she will come to me soon
and never leave.

She is heaven, she is what
no holy man or promise of salvation
can provide to be a part of a communion
with God; the great
harmonic is to find completion in eternal,
undying love with one woman,
for this man was created only for her,
and she will bring me heaven.

Hell is not a place
or a final destination,
it's the absence of my woman,
it's a temporary asylum for the lonely -
who require one other specific soul
to elevate them to true perfection,
taking us to the heaven we aspire to.

Angels can float by you wistfully in hell,
simply because you're still lonely
in the dark abyss, and the
Angels can sense your deepest sorrow.
There are Angels in hell,
there are Angels everywhere.

Heaven and hell are within;
only true love can determine
in which you'll live.

To the chagrin of the Bible thumpers,
God's love does not fulfill a soul in love
minus his mate, for God designed
these souls to be pristine lovers who
are for each other, not just to be.

My hell shall become heaven soon
for I will know what it is to be accepted,
loved, perfected and then I can truly
stand in Gods' eyes, not alone but
holding her hand.

"There are an infinite number of universes existing side by side and through which our consciousnesses constantly pass. In these universes, all possibilities exist. You are alive in some, long dead in others, and never existed in still others. Many of our "ghosts" could indeed be visions of people going about their business in a parallel universe or another time—or both."

—*PAUL F. ENO, Faces at the Window*

Parallel Universe

Conversation channeled from Jim Morrison

Jim: Rise up from the ashes,
You're a Ghost no more,
People can see you,
Shhhh, Shhhh, She's
coming this way,
She might see you

Other male voice: So?

Jim: Didn't anybody tell you
spirits aren't suppose to be
seen on earth? You'll
frighten them because
of what they've seen
on movies and TV

Other male voice: The quiet kid in the
dorm room at the elite college
isn't suppose to scare anyone,
though one day soon he'll
get a gun and blow himself
and six others away on campus

Jim: Yes but now the spirit world and earth
are suppose to be kept separate.
Everything on earth must be contained.
They think if a spirit is on earth, he doesn't
know he's dead right?

(Loud Laughter of two voices)

Other Male Voice: That's a good one, since the
Spirit can move around at the speed of light
to other dimensions and he ca be in two places
at the same time - but he's dead?

(More laughter of two voices)

Jim: And there they are in their human bodies,
with the human condition of aches and pains,
their diabetes, cancer, and the bum ticker
but they call themselves alive?

(One voice laughing)

Other Male Voice: How do they figure that?

Jim: Where is the wall between the spirit world and Earth? Where exactly is the divider? I can't see one.

Other Male Voice: I can't see one either....

Jim: So how do we know there is one?

CHAPTER 2

The Provocateurs

"I got to be Jim Morrison a lot longer than he did."

—*Warren Zevon*

Jim Morrison:

There is much speculation made by those of you on earth in what actually occurs when you return to this side. I am not here to end all the speculation or attempt to tilt your beliefs necessarily, however I will attempt to shed some light on the experience.

Have I met all, or most of the significance spiritual leaders and great philosophers who once walked on the earth on this side? The answer is, NO, I have not. Have I met some of my idols in Philosophy, Nietzsche? Rimbaud? The answer is, NO, I have not. Why you may ask? There are several reasons actually. When you ascend to this side, it's not as simple as having a wish list of who you'd like to meet, it must be agreeable to both parties.

For example, if you've dreamt of meeting J.F.K. and asking who shot him or having a few moments with Albert Einstein or someone more superfluous like Marilyn Monroe, you need to understand that Albert or Marilyn MUST also wish to be in your company and engage in communication. It's pretty much like making a phone call with a feature you now have on earth (caller I.D.) and if you chose to pick-up the phone and speak to that person, then the two-way conversation will occur and if not, you can leave a message. In other words, Albert or Marilyn will become aware you called, but they may not return the call as they may not have any desire to do so.

When you come to this side, there are no celebrities and no matter how famous you were on earth, there is no preferential treatment. Every soul has their own baggage and levels of enlightenment to ascend through. No one walks around and says "Oh my God, you're Jim Morrison" because when you come here, the shallow pool of fame is meaningless in this vast ocean. The only so-called famous souls I know from earth, are members of my primary soul group and I know far more souls who were never famous or wealthy on earth in terms of material goods.

I would have no desire if a fan of mine crosses over who wanted to meet me, to pick-up the phone or answer the call. It's not that I am being aloof, it's simply a question of the purpose, as my soul needs its actions to be purposeful and this would not seem like a meaningful or worthwhile communication for either of us.

I would however caution, that while you always have a choice on this side to whom you engage with in communication, be assured you will have to deal with each person you knew on earth and had relationships with once they cross over. You may need to make an apology, accept an apology, or have some sort of counseling to heal the relationship so both souls may either go their own way, or continue to be in touch and allow their relationship to evolve on this side. You will be brought before your family members, friends and enemies when they cross or when you cross if they are already here. You cannot be forced to apologize, make amends or heal but most souls I have communicated with on this side, wish to end their earth business in fair and truthful ways. You will not have to be engaged in communication with a casual friend or acquaintance, but with those you had significant relationships with.

As for me, I lead a very short, unhappy and painful existence. I have decided to heal each relationship with a family member or friend and move on to continue my work on this side; I will not be close to anyone from my past life and this is not because these souls are not interesting in their own way. On the contrary, I have simply chosen a different path away from that last life and onto new heights with my eternal soul mate when she returns home.

Most souls on this side, I should say any and all I have ever come in contact with, go to school, work or do both. I have yet to encounter an idle soul on this side and that is because each soul seems to be in the process of evolution and personal revolution. There are so many options on this side, it's important not to believe, each soul goes to the mystery schools if you have heard of them or each soul is helping others cross over or anything like that. There are schools and jobs here that I would suggest no one on earth has ever heard of or is yet aware of.

It's very individual and if you believe your schedule on earth is now hectic, it's nothing compared to what it's like here but you will be much more comfortable in the role of multi-tasking. You will not tire so easily, you will not be ruled by the clock and you will be fulfilled in what you are doing much more than what most of you are currently doing on earth. It's actually something to look forward to and not something to fear.

So why haven't I tried to communicate with Nietzsche or Rimbaud? For one reason, I no longer have any questions for them, I feel I now have the answers I long sought on earth. There are actually people walking around earth who sit on the major highway now (the internet) and spend their precious time on earth recounting of how they knew me. Some write books or contribute to articles and some, just plain brag. Not sure why they brag about such a thing. Claiming to know me and fifty cents won't even buy a cup of coffee these days.

While some of those who claim to have personally known me absolutely did, I find it fascinating and in some ways disturbing as to why they feel the desire or maybe even the need to recount our relationship to others, including complete strangers. I have finally come to the conclusion, they didn't truly get the piece of me they wanted. In other words, what I gave each of them wasn't enough or what they had hoped for because those who genuinely got a piece of me (so to speak) feel genuinely fulfilled to the point, they don't necessarily need to share it with the world. I was not good at maintaining relationships on earth and just about everyone knows that and I was at the end especially, emotionally disconnected to everyone and everything.

To stay emotionally connected to me, as I was on earth, has made me puzzled and yet, I own no part of it from this side. As an alcoholic, obviously so much of my former life was a blur during those years everyone is so excited about knowing me. There are women saying they were girlfriends of mine. Girlfriends? It's a question alright since they regard being around me once or twice publicly and spending a few nights giving me sex in a motel room the makings of any sort of relationship. Do they care I had 4 or 5 or more just like them at the same time? My single greatest sexual experience on earth was in fact with two strippers in L.A. one night when I wasn't drunk off my ass, just slightly buzzed. So I guess those who called themselves my "girlfriends" should realize, the emotional connection was not there, I am sorry, it never was.

The emotional connections I had to anything or anyone on earth were few and far between and were all over by the time I went to Paris. No woman really had me in that emotionally connected way and I think looking back, each and every one of them knew it because I was living moment by moment and had many moments without them even being on my mind. I felt an emotional connection to books at an early age, then to my written words in my poems throughout my short life. I felt this great energy dynamic when I was with the other Door's and when what we were doing was really on in a given night of a live performance. I use to find the studio tedious at times, all the unnecessary retakes were a complete drag for me but there were times we created something in the studio that was really superb and I felt an energy connection as the Door's were one body, not the four of us during those times.

The only other person I felt a real energy connection to as an adult was a man named Michael McClure. It was indescribable when I met him how I felt. It was a rare occurrence for me to feel so linked to someone, as in a kinship sort of way but with my friend Michael, I did. Michael and I had a soul connection and it was a relationship I truly valued. I felt I should've spent more time with Michael and done more work with him, as we were only getting started.

The truth has been held within my soul since 1971 and it's time to let it be known. My true emotional connection, the one I needed and wanted the most was on earth while I was on earth. She was however, only a little girl when I shed my skin and went into the so-called light. My eternal soul mate was my true emotional connection. I gave other women what I thought were pieces of me, they weren't really. I gave other women dramatic moments and pseudo-romance because there was truly only one woman for me that I came to earth to connect with. I ran through all the others and never found completion or satisfaction despite what people say. I needed this one woman to set me straight and reveal the real me so she could heal me, love me and embrace me. My darling Rebecca is my true emotional connection on earth. I love only her and I see, only her.

On this side while I wait patiently but mostly impatiently for Rebecca, I study and work to evolve and share things with her when she returns home. I hang-out with the famous from earth and the infamous. I hang-out with members of my soul group and some others and I wait for my woman.

There are no celebrities on this side. No one is special but those who have worked and evolved and have "ascended" are the ones that are revered and admired. You will find most of them, lived frugal lives. Not many of them were ever in the limelight on earth. Two cats I have become close to on this side you may have heard of are Dennis Wilson, of "The Beach Boys" and the true lyrical genius, Warren Zevon, of Warren Zevon.

Dennis and I were so much alike when we were on earth, it's almost frightening. Dennis is very at peace on this side and ponders over how his life got so wrecked and out of control like mine did. Dennis and I were of course, both extreme alcoholics who took insane chances to

conquer fear and feel alive. Dennis and I lived similar lives in many ways but he of course, was the genius behind one of my all-time favorite groups "The Beach Boys." I was always a big fan of the group and of his brother Brian. Dennis regrets doing one thing I didn't do, leaving behind so many kids but he feels they are better off only because, he was such a bad alcoholic.
In communicating with Dennis, I was surprised to learn, his proudest professional accomplishment was not "The Beach Boys" but a solo album he did called "Pacific Ocean Blue" which he would like all of his fans and cohorts on earth to know, captures the true spirit of Dennis Wilson. Dennis does like to go back to California and when he does, I do not accompany him. California is no longer my trip, I'm over it. My memories there are not so sweet but Dennis stays very connected to the place he lived and as you would say, died. I am good friends with Dennis now and found him to be a sort of magical soul. We aren't alcoholics anymore. We are just Jim and Dennis, free spirits.

Dennis was falsely accused of being involved in the "Manson Murders" because he knew old Charlie Manson. I was actually questioned about those murders while I was on earth, can you believe that? A man who had cut my hair in the infamous "young lion" style was a murder victim in those depraved acts. This man happened to be gay and made a pass at me the second time I saw him and I completely lost it with Jay. I have apologized to Jay on this side though we don't hang-out. Dennis Wilson was not involved with the Manson murders and never saw them coming when he knew Charlie. He knows more about Charlie than most people but those murders really messed with his mind. They had a deep and painful affect on him. He is really good on this side though, very well healed.

Another cohort of mine on this side is the mad genius known as Warren Zevon. I feel Warren Zevon is one of the greatest lyrical geniuses in American popular music. He wrote words that I see now are words I wish I would've said many times. Of course, Warren was more political than I was but we have so much in common besides alcohol. Warren use to draw much of his inspiration from books precisely as I did. We were both so inspired and transcended to new heights by books and great authors. Warren's use of the English language dazzles me and we are great comrades on this side.

Unbelievably, Warren felt a few times that he was living my life or something similar to my life on earth. He now knows that wasn't so, as he had some deep and meaningful love in his life. He has conveyed to me, that his "L.A. Woman" was a song called "The French Inhaler." I really love that song. I am honored to know Warren and to call him my friend. He wants everyone to know, he's not asleep and he's not dead, he's very much alive and well and he's still, the provocateur.

"Genius is the ability to put into effect what is on your mind."

—*F. Scott Fitzgerald*

There are two other friends of mine who are here and want to speak directly to my channel, in their own thoughts and words. I call them my two left-handed friends from Seattle. First I want to bring in Jimi Hendrix, a total musical genius and I wish I had known him better on earth. Jimi and I had a few straight conversations but generally I was pretty messed up when I ran into him. Contrary to what some claim, Jimi and I have not gone to any other channel in California or anywhere else and given our lyrics out. Jimi doesn't really have much desire to be channeled from this side but has decided to include his thoughts in this particular book.

Channel's note: I have been introduced to Jimi Hendrix previously and he has made his presence known to me at various times. He has also come through to some psychics for me to validate it is him, and he wants to channel in this book. I have no idea what he is going to say or talk about, much like Jim Morrison, it could be about anything but Jimi Hendrix is now coming through and I will take down his words, exactly as they are given to me. He feels quite high in vibration, he causes my ears to ring.

This world or the next

Channeled from Jimi Hendrix

Jimi shows me this quote:

And as he spoke of understanding, I looked up and saw the rainbow leap with flames of many colors over me. —Black Elk

Jimi Hendrix:

I'd like to say a few words, to my fans new and old and those who remember me. Thank you for wanting to remember me. I've come through from this side before but on a very limited occasion because I had to wait to find what I was searching for in a channel. This channel belongs to my illustrious soul group as it full of artists and volatile energies. I am not at this time or will not in the future be channeling to anyone else on earth. I have work I do here as a Spirit Guide and I am most happy with it. I

shall begin not at the beginning, but at the end.
But first, I give you these lyrics:

Mt. Shasta

Channeled from Jimi Hendrix

Sitting on Mt. Shasta,
On top of the Volcano,
all that nature is or will ever be,
is waiting to erupt

Saw the soul of the Motherland,
Saw the soul of the collective,
we are one body,
We all strike the same chord

Sitting on Mt. Shasta,
the rainbow now has 13 colors,
my eyes can hardly take in
what I see

Knowing this is where it began,
where it is and will end,
nothing so beautiful
as ever been known to me

The music under the earth
is the land of my birth,
on Mt. Shasta you can hear me,
you can feel me

Nature rumbles and awaits
it's great climax,
I want to be there when it happens,
As I am within the mountain
My motherland is Mt. Shasta,

My beginning, my end,
in Great Mt. Shasta
my color transcends and my music plays
on...forever

I died as you like to call it, from a drug overdose but if you want to know the truth, I was born because of that event. I'd say it was accidental on my part but you know, I had decided on a subconscious level or rather my soul decided, it was time to get the hell off of earth and return to paradise. I am telling you, I made the agreement to go home, or in your words, to die. I did this because I felt like I was suffocating on earth. I want to be clear cause this is my one real shot to get this right. I didn't go into that September night in London and take enough pills to intentionally end my life. I was actually having trouble sleeping and I was given those pills, in that amount by the woman with me. You can research who she was and why I chose not to say much about Monika is, she took her own life and is on this side trying to work things through, including the lies she told about me, our relationship and my death. Our relationship was short and I was really in a bad state when I met her.

I want to tell all of you, I didn't take those sleeping pills that night to kill myself on an intentional level but my soul was crying to go home. I absolutely asphyxiated on my own vomit, not a pretty picture but one I share with countless others over here. I went out rather violently at first but it became peaceful. The paramedics could not have saved my life. They were called too late and this is an area I have in common with Jim Morrison. Someone who supposedly loved us, didn't even know we were dead for sometime afterwards and lied and staged a cover-up to protect their own asses. It's rather tragic yet it's a metaphor for both of the lives we lived. Jim and I are really tight on this side now, despite we were mere acquaintances on earth. He was a genius and more of a poet than anyone gave him credit for but his soul was dying inside as was mine was, cause no one loved him.

I did have a great love in my life, her name was Kathy. She is my eternal soul mate without question and I was really fortunate to meet her. I was like a bad case of sunburn for her. The sun felt good and warm when you are laying on the beach but when you go home later, you hurt all over. This is what I was like to Kathy who I wrote "The wind cries Mary" for, since her middle name is Mary.

I had this trouble assimilating on earth, not so much due to the level of poverty I grew-up in and lived in most my life or the extreme culture of racism I experienced in my late teens and early 20's in America. But because I was spiritually gifted and could not so much as recognize what I had. I was what is now called an "Indigo child" not a "Voodoo Child" and I could see auras if I looked at you, between your eyes and stared for a few minutes. I didn't like what I saw in some of the folks around me but I didn't really understand why I could see auras and sometimes blobs of color.

I began experiencing vivid and wild dreams two years after my parents split up, when I was 11. I felt maybe it was due to living with my Cherokee Grandmother but I now realize, it was being around her energy and power that brought my spiritual gifts out more than before. I would see these colors my eyes could hardly register and they didn't seem to be like the colors I would see on earth. It was almost like I was traveling to other galaxies and seeing things that didn't even exist on earth. Whatever that world was, I longed not to wake from it or return to the life I led on earth. I always wanted to go back but would only recall going there a few times a year and always while asleep. I was actually doing what you call astral travel. I was leaving my body at night and going to other dimensions and it was one of these so-called dreams that inspired "Purple Haze." Now I realize, I wasn't dreaming, I was out of my body looking at other dimensions.

One of the reasons I chose to use LSD other than the typical one of it was the 60's and it was time to experiment had more to do with finding that world again and see if I could enter it through a drug trip. It didn't exactly work but I did like things on LSD more than I did when I was off it. Everything seemed more colorful, more beautiful and it was almost like the world should be in the colors all the time I saw while under the influence of the drug. I wanted to be in the other world, the one of my dreams.

My entire life was obviously about music. I poured my soul into playing the guitar which was almost too natural for me without formal training. I poured all that I was, into the music I created and I came to earth to transcend race with the one harmonic that joins all of us together, which is music. Nothing else can break down cultural walls, dissolve religious differences or erase racial lines like music has, can and will. I was here as Jimi Hendrix, an American of a mixed racial background at one of the most influential times in American History in regards to ethnicity to break down the walls and to represent the soul of a real American. America was this melting pot and I was fairly racially melted. I gained respect of all races eventually and more so of those in other countries than my own before I left the confines of my human body. America has come to recognize what I was trying to do and has given me beautiful tributes. I think it's important to recognize who I was in my poverty, my lack of primary parental home, my failure to finish High School, my difficult racial uprising, but my determination to become what I did as a musician and as a true American. On this side, of course we are not such nationalists but what I came to do was, harmonize all humanity but allow people to see a true American.

I performed "The Star Spangled Banner" as a true American, I felt it—I felt it all through my body, my soul and my heart. It was my America and as we look back, perhaps the America more people can resonate with because the National Anthem didn't sound a certain way, because it didn't have to. It could sound like I played it.

I came to earth to stand for all America was supposed to stand for. My greatest education on the state America was in, occurred in two areas. One was when I toured what they called the Chitlin Circuit, concurrently I fell in love with the blues and gained so much from that experience, I got some very blatant scenes of racism entrenched in the corners of my mind. The other was being a member of the United States Army. I was a poor soldier and I'll never deny it. I didn't want to be there because I lived for playing music, not for doing the dirty work of the government.

I was anti-war and remain anti-war because when you invade another's land you need to ask yourself, did this forceful, violent invasion make things worse or better? There comes a day your losses are too great and you have to leave and then what happens? There is this thing called karma, so foreign to most Americans and when you take another life, even in wartime to supposedly protect your own, you incur this thing called karma with the soul of that person you killed in the name of war and it has to be worked out. You can't really kill anybody because you can't kill their soul so you have to deal with all the things you did to everybody and taking a human life is a huge amount of karma to work out. Their soul and your soul are now cosmically joined and taking lives is not on any soul path, you chose to do that. Once you make that choice you are off your path and you have all this karma you have to contend with. Nothing you do on earth doesn't have what I would call soul consequences. You will deal with everything you did whether it was positive or negative and I have yet to see a soul on this side sitting around sipping a drink on a gorgeous beach. Souls work very hard on this side and the more karma you incur, the more work you're gonna have to do. The best advice I can give is, live by the golden rule, do unto others as you would have them do unto you.

There are many myths about me just as there are many truths. When it comes to drugs, yes, I used and enjoyed psychedelic drugs. I was without a doubt addicted to marijuana. Weed was a vice for me and while I believe it can be used like anything else in moderation, too much of it really does play havoc on the short term memory. I think the human race should rethink that marijuana is any worse for anyone than alcohol. I was a very peaceful man but for the times I was drunk.

Alcohol would make me violent, and half out of my mind. I was a horrible drunk and I never met anyone on earth who was helped by being drunk. No one is creative when drunk, or even descent. You either become violent, stupid so you can become a victim or do something you could regret in the morning if not all your life, or you become pathetic and not someone anyone wants to be around. Alcohol was something I should've avoided at all costs. I could be creative on other drugs but never on alcohol. I could be respectful and decent on other drugs and turn out half out of my mind when I drank. Alcohol is legal in the United States and nothing good ever comes out of it. People can write and create on other drugs but can't do anything of any use on alcohol. There are too many damn drunks in the United States, crying in their sorrows and not enough people creating and reformulating the definition of what it is to be an American. I am not advocating drug use from this side because I did too much and it wasn't always good for me. I am merely pointing out the discrepancy in all of it. Alcohol is legal and socially acceptable and weed isn't? Why?

Many believed near the end of my days I was becoming increasingly paranoid from all my drug use. It just so happens, I had a right to be paranoid. If I stayed on earth another year, it seems more than likely I would've been a murder victim. People who had been playing with my money would've chosen to silence me. I was unaware of their deep organized crime connections or what was really taking place. I now am aware I would've been snuffed out if I had continued on.

I was busted for having drugs on me in London at the airport and I was later acquitted. I wasn't dumb enough to do that. The heroin was placed in my bag by someone I know it turns out. I was lucky to be acquitted on that charge and I know that. I am grateful I wasn't railroaded.

This is where my life intersects with two others in my soul group, Jim Morrison and Michael Hutchence. Starting with Jim, I never understood him on earth. He was a lush and a bad one at that. I would look at this prima donna, who looked like a Greek God for a time and never got as bad looking as people said. He was handed this career. I had to work my ass off to get a gig for years, play in places Morrison would never have to and never saw much money. Morrison practically walked into his opportunity and I can't say he wasn't talented, but he was also the white pin-up boy for a hysterical race of sexually repressed adolescent girls.

I resented Morrison for what he was handed on earth. The last time I saw him wasn't during that now famously recorded jam session featuring him yelling obscenities over my guitar work. I saw him again in a private moment and it was not for long but he had lost his life force. His soul was dying and I could tell. I saw a man that had it all handed to him but didn't know what to do with it and was unaware of the power he had.

I also knew this then and can confirm it now. Jim Morrison was dying from a lack of love. He didn't love himself but he didn't love anybody else either. He was just walking through life minute by minute but I could tell he had no real soul mate. I saw him with different women at different times and knew some women who had been with him. I knew for a fact he had no soul mate. He couldn't hold it together so it all fell apart. One of the first things that happened when we reunited on this side was, Jim showed me his eternal soul mate still walking the earth. I never saw anybody with more regrets about leaving anyone else behind. He was a loner on earth but he is tired of being alone now.

My other brother here is Michael Hutchence and I want to say this, he was a helluva lot more talented than anyone has ever given him credit for. He had the charisma and whether you liked the music he sang or not there is no one to compare to his stage presence. Jim, Michael and I share an interesting dynamic. We were all falsely accused of something we didn't do. Jim was thought to have exposed himself in Miami and he didn't. I thought he probably did it on earth, because he was really obscene and out of it on stage at times. It turns out, people assumed he did it because he was Jim Morrison. People also assumed that Michael Hutchence had drugs in the house of his girlfriend Paula Yates and when her house was busted for drugs, he was to blame. It turns out this was not so, but because Michael was such a party boy, it was assumed to be so. Because I did so many drugs, it was assumed the drugs found in my bag at the airport were mine. They weren't. Jim Morrison, Michael Hutchence and I found ourselves surrounded in false accusations while we were on earth. This is not a coincidence and our own actions brought about these accusations. We put ourselves out there and we all knew the political climate of when and where we lived. We knew there were people always out to get us. Michael, who had his problems in London like me, also knew at the time the London media was out to hang him and inevitably, he hung himself (no pun intended).

We were targets, but you know we made ourselves easy targets. I will admit to trying heroin but I didn't like the trip. I didn't see how anyone could be creative on that shit and I also hated needles. It's actually humorous so many people falsely claim Jim Morrison and I were into heroin and neither one of us were at all. We both hated needles and someone shot me up in London and man, I was sick as a dog and never could understand anyone's attraction to that sick shit. I hated it and I had an autopsy, so maybe the know it alls should check and see if any heroin was found in my body. If I was an addict, what happened, did I give it up that quickly and the needle marks just magically vanished?

I had a thing for RAINBOWS because I was the rainbow. The rainbow colors just happen to coincide with the seven chakras or energy centers of the body. It's not a coincidence as my music was there to cause vibration in all seven energy centers of the body.

I had many influences all through my life and they have been much to my surprise, well documented. Of course B.B. King, Muddy Waters, T-Bone, Albert King, Elvis, Little Richard and on and on were great influences on me. I liked to learn from any and all musicians because if music was also there passion, there was also something to be learned. Little Richard made this impact on me as a stage performer because the crowd would never be bored watching him. The guitar was simply an extension of my human body, and I played it as I felt it inside. I hoped the crowd could never be bored listening or watching me.

Some of the people who meant the most to me in my lifetime include Frank Zappa. He not only introduced me to the famous wah wah peddle but he said something to me that changed how I thought and felt and sometimes, someone can just say two or three lines and they can mean more to you than the long dialogues you have with others. Frank was a musical genius and we are very close on this side. I have a great love for Arthur Lee. I have this true admiration for a singer on this side now named Jeff Buckley. I have a real affection for James Brown over here now. The stars on earth don't hang together over here but the music draws us in and our passion for it. My favorite band probably was and remains "The Who." I have a deep love for Eric Clapton, always will. He gets better with age but he appreciates the artistry of others and has such great respect for it.

I do have biological children on earth. I am not going to tell you who they are or where they are, because it will seem strange to some of you yet this communication is as natural to me as playing the guitar was on earth. My children are victims of circumstance and I was aware of one son before I came home. I was planning to acknowledge him and hoped to find some way to be in his life somehow. He was on my mind and the others I didn't actually know about on earth. I am sorry I left them behind. I wouldn't have been much of a Father on earth but I do watch over them here and am a better Father to them from where I am. I know that's not how it should be, but it's how it is.

My soul was ready to come home. Once that occurs, the body wants to separate from it. I could've gone out in a variety of different ways but I don't particularly like the way I went. I was having a really bad dream, a terrible nightmare and I was struggling and fighting in this dream and then it was over. I am at a peace and I have worked extremely hard on this side to evolve and become a Spirit Guide. I still play my music, but now can play many different instruments and create sounds you can't create on earth. I have a passion for change on earth and I tell all of you, to use music to transcend all races. Take someone like Mozart or Beethoven, people of all lands and all persuasions know this music and have for hundreds of years. Music is timeless, music is pure love and it's the thread each human being has in common. A song like "Silent Night" is known throughout the world. While you are singing "Silent Night" just imagine who else is singing it and where they are. Music is the one single thing that can harmonize the entire world yet as powerful as it is, people simply use it for money instead of creating the vibrations of the universe with it, seeing the rainbow. Music, sweet music is the greatest single gift mankind has. I am glad to have contributed what I could to music; I was honored to share my rainbow. I was ready to go back to where I belong. My life wasn't cut short but please let me be known for sharing my soul with each of you.

What's in your voodoo bag?
Channeled from Jimi Hendrix

Magic stones, essential oils,
clutter your voodoo bag,
the tools you think you need
aren't really tools at all -

but fools buy into exterior
forces without realizing
the power they have
within them...

The sun is in my voodoo bag,
yes the sun,
the moon is in my voodoo bag,
yes the moon,
the stars are in my voodoo bag,
yes the stars....

A touch of lightning
and the summer's rain
give my bag all the voodoo
that it needs...

My soul is magical
and nature is my
spell caster....

Open my bag and see
the thirteen colors of the rainbow....

Open my bag and notice
there are 13 signs in the zodiac....

My bag is for real Shaman,
the high priests of the Temple,
not for someone using a deck
of tarot cards and putting
spells on your lover...

My voodoo bag is mine
and not like any other...
I've got divine magic
through and through...

So what's in your voodoo bag?
How does it show me - you?

Jim Morrison:

I have this other friend, also from Seattle, also was a left-handed friend like Jimi Hendrix but this guy learned to use his right hand. He wants to be heard now, because he has this crazy fan base, somewhat like mine but he'll tell you, his is larger (Smiles). With no further adieu, my friend, Kurt Cobain.

Channel's note: Kurt Cobain has introduced himself to me before from the other side at first while I was in the bathroom. I have a rule of no spirit communication while I am in the bathroom and yet this male voice came through talking to me while I was washing my hands. He told me he was Kurt and a friend of Jim's. At first, I genuinely had no idea who he was but through time, his communication skills with me seemed to have gotten stronger. I am honored to take down his words and give you his exact communication.

Memoria

Channeled from Kurt Cobain

Quote from Kurt Cobain while he was on earth:

"I really haven't had that exciting of a life. There are a lot of things I wish I would have

done, instead of just sitting around and complaining about having a boring life. So I pretty much like to make it up. I'd rather tell a story about somebody else."

Kurt Cobain:

What difference does it make how I did it? I was in the midst of killing myself for years before it ended but you called it art. Art equals the music of a dying man.

You said you related to me. I guess you were dying too. Or were you living in way that felt like you were dying? You related to what about my music or about me? That you didn't fit in either?

That everybody wrote you off because you lived under a bridge? Some say I never lived under that bridge, isn't where you spend most of your time where you live? Maybe you got your ass kicked for the hell of it like I did. But you rose up and sang your songs all to realize you were too sensitive and nobody got you like you thought they would. My point is, I guess some of my life was somewhere in the memory of your life. One day you were going to do something big and show them who you were.

There was no cure for who I was. It was a destiny's whose volume turned up to tragedy from the start. Everyone wants to know how I died. Does it matter because you think my murderer is walking around? What if my murderer was fame? Fame doesn't fit everyone. It's the wrong size and wrong color for some of us.

I'll tell you what I have come to say. I was leaving that day. I was leaving everybody behind and everything to start anew. I didn't think I was going to get this kind of a fresh start when I made up my mind. The reports I wasn't leaving anybody are lies. I was leaving everybody. The only one I wanted to continue to see and be close to was my F.B. (my beautiful Francis), the apple of my eye.

Just so you know, I don't like psychics. Most are phony, or too impressed with themselves. This channel doesn't want to be a psychic. I watch her and see she's almost embarrassed by it. That's why I like her. She's not comfortable in her own skin. I know how she feels, so I talk to her. I hang around my daughter, and I talk to this channel. I won't be coming in for others now because it's this big energy pull, and I don't want that. My energy is intense and it makes this channel dizzy sometimes. She feels me. I don't like the fact she wants to lay on the floor and vomit from this vertigo state I put her in, but it's a cool relationship. I don't really like psychics but for her.

Psychics bore me. The ones who claim to talk to Jesus or some holy entity would try and say I am not evolved or a lower energy. Why? Cause I was in a rock band, and I stuck a needle in my arm? They judge me, and I wonder if they could feel the constant pain I had in my stomach, would a needle be in their arm? Or would they justify their righteous selves by taking prescription drugs? The holier than thou psychics are hypocrites. There are ones who think someone shouldn't channel the dead. You should hang-up your shingle, you charlatan. We aren't dead, and I also dislike the term "disembodied beings." The human body is just like taking off a coat. You hang-up the coat or throw it on the floor, whichever, but you are still you. So to the psychics who read this and don't like it, I am sticking out my middle finger.

Are they better than me? Where did they grow-up? Did their Father hit them in private and in public? The drugs were a cosmic catastrophe but I'm here to talk about some other stuff I want to comment on.

If you met me right now, what would you say? Would you ask mc how I died or why I lived? Do you know your life shouldn't come down to one day - the day you said Bon Voyage Cruel World because it's never about one day. It's about all the days and all the ways you loved others and gave them pieces of your soul. I did give parts of my soul away when I sang, when I wrote. Would I do it again? No, I want to be in that garden with Jim Morrison. The garden where all the dead bodies are buried but can be resurrected.

I wouldn't come back as Kurt Cobain. I wouldn't live that life again and hope to achieve a different outcome. It cost me too much but the price wasn't high enough. "Hey Jude, take a sad song and make it better." Take the pain I lived in and let it out. No one should live in that pain. Let it out however you must "then you can begin to make it better."

I was dead for three years before I died. I was more dead than I am now. George Romero should've made a movie about me. Did I take my own life? Does it matter now? I did what I did and you know I was killing myself. Yes, I took my own life but you were right to think there was some tampering with things and it didn't go down like they said it did. I was gone on the heroin. I wasn't aware so it's a good time to implicate, but it's not a good time to implicate because I have a child. I will always put my daughter first but she'll ask questions—more questions than before in a few years and realize I did it but things were altered afterwards. They had to be altered in someone's estimation. They had to be made more substantive because the drugs were messing with everybody's mind around me. The drugs made squares into triangles and circles into squares. They really had a square in front of them but viewed it as a triangle.

If I told you I did it, I did it, but there was some stuff done afterwards like the note I supposedly left behind in that form, that people should continue to question. Did I leave a "suicide note?" No, I didn't. Insanity doesn't enable a person to write a note. I was insane, filled with physical and psychological pain. I was given a death sentence at birth. It's just that, some of you heard of me. You wanted to hear of me.

Chemical imbalance causes intestinal grief, but the doctors never figured it out. I was a born with a severe Chemical Imbalance; most people only have a slight one. I could've become a serial killer with how screwed up my brain was, but I really did feel things for other people and could never descend into that. When I was young, I did some things to animals I look back on and know it was vile. I'm sorry for that. I am sorry for your pain. I am sorry for my pain. I conquered that desired tendency to hurt someone. I only hurt myself, my daughter and you, I guess.

I had a hard time crossing over, really hard time. One of the first ones that helped me over here was Jim Morrison. He was and is really good to me and I realize now, he was brave. He drank too much but he would've never taken his own life. He would always think there was hope. I felt trapped. I felt trapped cause of this record deal that didn't play out and should've. I felt trapped because I didn't think anyone understood what I was doing musically and personally. I felt trapped by the drugs. I felt trapped by the stomach pain, the emotional pain, all of it. I felt like an animal in a hunter's trap. I'm so free now, no more pain, no more distortion of the truth. No more distortion.

If other psychics believe I have spoken to them (cough, cough), they should've heard me mention the name Michael Hutchence. Hutch and I are very close on this side. He was a big fan of mine on earth and I am a big fan of his in death (Laughs). Hutch has been a true support to me and even though I came over here before he did, he has evolved more. His soul level or vibration is higher than mine because I have more to do than he did. His soul is restored and mine will hopefully be at some point.

So much has been written about me and calculated about the position of the gun and who actually pulled the trigger. Where was Lee Harvey Oswald that day? I would laugh about it but it's almost sad in a way. Why do I have to be this clinical case study?

Everyone might be waiting for me to say something about Courtney. That will be done in private. I will tell her when I see her. I'm grateful for this opportunity because, this communication is not all that easy for me. I would tell you I'd work on it but, never mind. I don't want to try and be understood anymore. Does that make sense?

Red Roses

Channeled from Kurt Cobain

Rose are red
They bleed in your garden
The Roses are dead
They wilted last night

The Roses are bleeding
So alive in my garden
The Roses died again
Their petals are all over my face

Red Roses for her
Red Roses for me
I gave up bringing her roses
I got over my disease

I think I'm over my disease
You brought me Red Roses
to honor the dead
I was standing right behind you

Why'd you put them on the ground?
Why not hand them to me instead?

As the petals scatter
Remember one thing
You can't give roses to a dead man
I'm not dead

Why don't you hand them to me?
I was dead for three years on earth
Now I'm alive, I'm so alive
What do you think about that?

Red Rose rarely talk -
This guitar rarely sleeps

Refuge
Channeled from Kurt Cobain

I have no refuge from the rain
pouring down...
I have no refuge from this old,
dirty town...

The bodies are hidden everywhere,
and as you just stop and stare,
you say nothing, you just keep
on walking by...

I have no refuge from the way I left
things with you...
I can't come back and take it all way,
and you know it would never do...

the bodies are hidden everywhere,
and sometimes when you see nothing

but the glare,
I am there, but you just keep on walking by...

I have no refuge like I thought I would find,
and when I was there I just wasted all my time...
Nothing else can hold me down,
I should've stayed around, but I thought
there was refuge without you...

I wanted to leave it all behind and find some
refuge in my mind
but I just wasted all my time...
Was I a waste of your time?
You couldn't fix me...
So why do you miss me?
And I thought there
was refuge without you

I don't have refuge
because I should've said goodbye...
but who would understand the reasons why...
No one knew, I was through with you...
I have no refuge so you can dry your eyes
and you can keep on, keep on walking

CHAPTER 3

Heavenly Brilliance

"Color has taken possession of me; no longer do I have to chase after it. I know that it has hold of me forever... Color and I are one. I am a painter."

—*Paul Klee*

The Songbird

Jim=Jim Morrison
Jac=Jacqueline Murray (Channel)
Eva=Eva Cassidy

Jim: I wanted to introduce you to someone over here, who is very special to me and many others on earth at this time. She is really extraordinary and she is not the type to necessarily be channeled but I think there are some messages she wants to pass along.

Jac: Ok I'm ready

Eva: Hello Jacquie, my name is Eva Marie Cassidy. It's nice to meet you.

Jac: I know who you are, I am so honored to meet you. I am much more familiar with some of your music than that of the others that have come in.

Eva: Thank you, I know who you are (smiling), I already consider you a friend. I have been told about you, mostly from Hutch (Michael Hutchence).

Jac: Oh you hang-out with Michael?

Eva: Yes, we have become pretty close. We teach classes for children. We play guitars, we sing and we paint and create with them Jacquie. It's wonderful. Hutch and I teach classes and we flourish here being around the young ones.

Jac: that's amazing Eva. I really love your singing. I love your rendition of "Over the Rainbow" and your versions of "Time After Time" and "Fields of Gold."

Eva: Thank you Jacquie. I wanted to give a few messages if I may?

Jac: I am really humbled and honored.

Eva: So am I. I'm filled with gratitude that my music has I guess you'd call it taken on a fan base now (Smiles). I really didn't want to be famous on earth Jacquie. I was scared to death of it. I know this is going to sound weird but I liked being relatively obscure. I didn't want the intrusion. I was a really private person and I couldn't see having to answer questions or not being able to just go off and ride my bike or paint or something. My music was meant to be left behind, so it could be found after I left. Do you understand this?

Jac: I think so, fame isn't for everybody.

Eva: No and it wasn't for me. I couldn't help but to sing. I couldn't stop myself. I felt the voice was coming from a different place though. When I would really get into the song, I felt it was coming from I don't know, but I now know God gave me this incredible gift. It wasn't perfect but it was a gift. Sometimes I would see colors when I sang.

Jac: Well your voice was and I am sure still is, amazing.

Eva: Thank you, I constantly sing over here. I can't stop singing. I sing for God, for the universe, for all there is. I was this intensely private and shy girl and I see so much of me in you because you are private and somewhat shy and I know this is not what you had in mind to do with your life (talk to singers from the other side).

Jac: No not at all.

Eva: I did something that I want to talk about in my life. I honored the artist within. There were lots of times I didn't feel I was good enough or a vocal I did wasn't good enough. I worried too much about it being perfect or a certain way and I wish I would've gotten over that but I lived this quiet, peaceful life and just sang and painted. I worked in a nursery. There is no more precious and tranquil place to go day in and out. But my music dominated and I couldn't keep myself from singing even with all the stage fright I had sometimes or the critical nature of feeling my vocals were not as on as they could've been. I didn't want to be a star or be famous. I just honored my gift and I liked to perform in front of small crowds. What began to get to me toward the last years of my life, was how I saw the affect my vocals or interpretation of the song had on people. That touched my soul so deeply and I am so grateful for that.

There are many people who helped and supported me and had more faith in me than I had in myself. My Dad started the whole thing (Smiling) with me singing but my family was supportive and wonderful and my manager was a rock but it was Chris who really made it so people would hear my music now. I owe him so much. I am so grateful to him and have a deep love for him always. We were romantically involved once but it was not meant to be. We were meant to be the greatest friends and he is a real genius when it came to cultivating my work in studio.

Jim: Eva and I have something very deep in common. We both never got to meet our eternal soul mates on earth.

Eva: My friendship with Jim Morrison may seem really strange to some but Jim is actually pretty shy and sensitive. When I sing over here, he would be there listening and I really don't feel as if people on earth got to know him, not on a soul level.

Sadly, I had cancer all throughout my body. It was devastating because I was young and healthy I thought and couldn't really comprehend something like that spreading so quickly. I hope that somehow, young women learn from me. I had this skin cancer removed from my back at one point and I thought it was done and I was fine. I didn't understand how some cancers can spread and grow and how much it can affect a younger person.

If I could've stayed, I would've met him in less than a year (my soul mate that is). I would've been 34 when I met him and by 35, we'd never be apart. He's still on earth and like Jim, I have to watch him as Jim watches his life partner and sometimes it's so hard but I live with the knowledge and the blessing that he is going to return to me someday soon and we won't be apart.

Jac: That's so beautiful Eva and in some ways, so sad. Does he know of you Eva?

Eva: Yes, he knows he is drawn to my voice but can't figure out why he becomes so emotional when he hears me sing. I don't sing his type of music or at least the type he use to listen to. Someone popped my CD in while they were driving somewhere and I was happy he didn't tell the woman to take it out. He listened to it. He heard me and has been listening ever since.

Jac: WOW, that's amazing.

Eva: Like Jim Morrison, I didn't make that connection on earth. While I can't wait to see him face to face, I want him to have a happy life. I just know it will be so sweet when we meet on this side.

Jac: I will be happy for you Eva when that happens. May I ask you a question?

Eva: Of course Jacquie.

Jac: Did you have a favorite song that you recorded while on earth?

Eva: I have a few, but there are songs I wish I had recorded on earth, many of those. I really was an acoustic girl, but now a part of me would have liked to hear my voice with a whole, large arrangement. I can do so many things on this side that I couldn't do on earth so my imagination has no limit. I have mixed feelings about the work I left behind but I am so grateful I wasn't forgotten and I cherish those who helped bring it more to the forefront. I would not have done that on earth and they know it.
Many have done beautiful recordings of "Imagine" but I think from where I am now, I relish that I got to record that song. I think it's

about heaven. It sums it all up. I have many I love but I feel I did a really great version of "the letter" (Smiles) and for some reason I fondly look back on that now. I love "Over the Rainbow" but there are some many who have done outstanding versions of that song. There are two ladies on earth who I think have fabulous versions, Jane Monheit and Linda Eder. Of course Judy Garland's is the stand out.

I wish I had recorded quite a few songs. The list is really long but I sing them over here. I never really wanted to do any Door's songs (smiles) but if I did one, it would be "Spanish Caravan" because I really do like that song.

Jim: Thank you.

Eva: I don't want anyone to think I have regrets of not being known while I was on earth or not getting to do this or that. I am happy with the life I had. At the end, in those final weeks, the outpouring of love for me was so overwhelming I am still spinning from it over here. My family, my friends, even strangers were wonderful and I could not have asked for a better send-off. I would hate to say the highpoint of my life was the send-off. It was singing of course songs like "Imagine" but I can't deny the uplifting love I felt in those final weeks. I was lifted to heaven, literally.

Jac: That's so beautiful Eva.

Eva: I was not a religious person, not into reading the Bible but I was spiritual in my own way. I paint Angels over here and on this side, my paintings are even more than three dimensional because I learned angels surrounded me on earth and they surround me here. Their beauty is unmatched and also their uniqueness. They are like snowflakes, no two look the same.

I know that people will think some dead singer is talking about Angels, that's silly. Angels are sent by God to help us and guide us. They are ever present and there is nothing I can quite compare their beauty to. They have given me comfort, love and strength I didn't realize while on earth. Before I went home from the cancer, I began to see them and wondered if I was hallucinating. They took my pain away and carried me to heaven. I sing with the Angels now, what could be better than that?

Jac: Nothing I can imagine

Eva: I wanted to mention that I will send pink roses, pale pink roses around those I love at certain times. It's my signal. It's to tell them I love them, I am looking down on them and thank you.

Jac: Eva, you are such a beautiful soul surrounded in light, thank you for this.

Eva: Thank you Jacquie, I mean truly. You are a wonderful clear channel and where I am now is a wonderful world. The colors here are what I would never want to give up. So many more colors than I saw on earth, it's like the expanded box of crayons you can only dream about.

Jim: Jacquie, you know Eva and I were talking and we know there will be people on earth who trash this work and even trash you. Those are people we have to say, we don't care if they see the work, they are doing us no homage by keeping a closed mind.

Eva: It's unfair to condemn something they have never read. They should at least read it and then draw their own conclusions.

Jim: There is always someone who wants to rain on someone else's parade. They want to say this isn't possible because half of them probably wish we were talking to them or because their minds are too narrow for what I was trying to do on earth in the first place. I was always curious about this side, so why
wouldn't I communicate from it?

Eva: On the other hand (smiles) I was and still am, very private. I guess I'm locked in my own box. But I am grateful for the appreciation my singing has been receiving and really surprised. I wanted to thank everyone. I didn't really want to go to certain famous psychics. Nothing against them but they are showy and I wasn't into that and I'm not into it at all now. I'm just me (smiles).

Jac: For that, we are all grateful Eva.

Jim: We just want you to know what you are doing is a really valuable thing for all of us and we chose you for specific reasons.

Eva: There is always someone negative, someone who tries to hold you back and clip your wings somewhere. I never understood that energy Jacquie and never wanted to be around it. I lived such a quiet, peaceful existence and it was partially because that energy was not something I could probably handle. You have a gift and you have chosen to use it. You are helping us and those who read this we hope. I would hope others would focus on their gifts, and embrace them and not put yours down.

Jac: Thank you, I don't really get caught-up in negativity. I don't read the reviews or comments. I don't have time for one thing and the energy is not worth exhausting on it.

Jim: (Clapping hands) here, here. Some people love to poison your mind with their careless and corrosive words. We have no room for that.

Eva: Jacquie thank you again, it was real honor.

Jac: The honor was mine, thank you Eva.

Jim: I would now like to bring in my true soul brother, Michael Hutchence. He is going to talk about some of the hidden truths of the after life.

Channel's Note: Michael Hutchence the former lead singer of INXS has given me his words and thoughts on the afterlife.

Buried Treasure

Channeled from Michael Hutchence

As I look back, the painful realizations of
my tragic mistakes surround me...
and when I really stop and think
of them, they never cease to
astound me...

Where did all the time go?
The time I wasted away
I slept too many hours
and hid myself too many days

I didn't honor the sunlight
by spending enough time
in the rays, I didn't honor
the moonlight because
I stayed inside too much
and played

My soul wants to tell you
the truth it has learned,
life is very short dear one
to whom it may concern
Time is a precious gift

one you can't get back,
fill it with the sunshine,
the sweet smell of flowers,
the beautiful ocean and there
will be nothing that you lack

The pressures, the bills,
the squabbles and the drama,
are wasted hours,
as is any sort of trauma

Live each moment in the
most natural, simple way
and you won't go to
the other side, longing for
another day on earth,
for a new rebirth, you will
have enjoyed the simple pleasures,
and won't feel the need
to search for buried treasure

Michael Hutchence:

I would like to share my perceptions of the after life. I have said all I wanted to say about my life and death in the book "A TALE OF TWO BROTHERS: Jim Morrison and Michael Hutchence" by this channel, Ms. Jacqueline Murray. There are stories of me being around others on earth. I have been around a lovely young woman in Australia named Kassandra, and I urged her to read the two brothers book for a variety of reasons. I am also visiting on rather sporadic occasions, some of my friends on earth because I want them to know, this is real and understand, I am healed and I am whole, living in the light. So let me begin to detail what I came to share this time.

How can it be, that we ascend from heaven and are created there but lock ourselves in a living hell on earth? We are not born into hell, on the contrary, even with the worst circumstances of lack of parental love or caring, we are born of the light as our souls are pure light. How then, do we cage ourselves into this prison of hell on earth?

We are inundated at an early age by images of a culture that truly has no soul, let alone any sort of light beaming from it. We are to believe, that the perfect image for a woman can be found in something such as a Barbie doll or the latest issue of "Playboy" magazine instead of let's say the depiction of the Goddess Venus in a Paolo Caliari masterpiece! We are to believe "having it all" literally means having the hot girlfriend or boyfriend, lots of money, a fast car that turns heads, not to mention a somewhat perfect or close to perfect body. Why is it then, so many with the hot girlfriend or boyfriend, the nice car, the gorgeous dwellings to rest and play in and the disposable cash find themselves in drug rehab or even worse, on the brink of suicide? The superficial provides a temporary and somewhat hollow state of euphoria. It's like a drug trip, it doesn't last and you always wake-up, rather tired, irritable or somewhat disoriented.

On this side, there are many in my primary soul group who were and still are very talented artists of all kinds. Some were rather famous and some, you have never heard of. One of the blokes that crossed over that I recognized from a past existence was rather famous and he was known to the world as Heath Ledger. He is a brother of mine in various ways and just like me and the musical icon Kurt Cobain, Heath left behind a young daughter and he could not regret it more.

Someday, Heath will channel to the world, as he has much to say. He is in a phase of healing and dealing with his deep remorse but he does want his loved ones and fans to know, his passing was purely accidental. He was not at all suicidal and did not intend to leave his baby daughter or the earth the day he did which happened to have been on January 22nd, which was indeed my birthday on earth.

Heath simply did what so many do and I was also guilty of. He mixed combinations of medications and just because so many have done it numerous times before, they believe there is no real danger. I can assure you that could not be further from the truth.

He actually mixed mostly his prescription medications and fell into a deep sleep. His immune system was compromised and despite the fact his autopsy did not report any pneumonia in his body, he was suffering from what could be termed walking pneumonia not long before his passing. When you are physically ill and run down, it's quite easy not to pay attention to the pills you are mixing or the amount you are taking. He did not do this intentionally, he was accustomed to mixing medications and he admits, toward the end of his earth life, his soul was somewhat lost and seeking direction. He was not however, suicidal and he is filled with remorse. Like me and Kurt Cobain, he will have to suffice at being a doting Father from this side, which in many ways, is a beautiful sentiment but a very, very sad and difficult road.

Nevertheless, Heath feels the best thing he did in his earthly existence, was to have his daughter with his beautiful love, Michelle. There is no film or work he is more proud of, than the bright life he fathered while on earth.

So how it is a young man with everything to live for could end up like Heath Ledger? Self-loathing plays a great part in the demise of an artist as it did for me. The shy, sensitive soul is seen by others in more provocative ways that are not truly authentic to one's character. The world may see you as a more dynamic talent than you see yourself.

It's not a coincidence that Heath Ledger did a video shoot prior to his passing for a great artist named Nick Drake. Heath and Nick were very much and I should say, are very much alike. I have had the great pleasure of getting to know the very talented Nick Drake on this side as well. Heath and Nick are truly kindred spirits. An artist is capable of going down so low, to the absolute bottom of the barrel so to speak and this is where his greatest work often arises from. Not from the good times, not from the temporary euphoria obtained from drugs, alcohol or sex but from the ebbs of destruction, when we step back and look into the abyss of pain, we will often create our very best works. To write, to paint, to draw, or to compose a song, are much better ways to deal with depression than any pill or psychotherapy. Your soul cries out to be authentic. An artist who does his or her art for the sake of commercial success will probably need that pill or psychotherapy, they are not creating from the very depths of who they are, or what they feel. In our deepest feelings, we find God, we find truth.

Wasn't it Jesus who cried out on the cross "Father, why have you abandoned me?" We all at some point feel abandoned, alone and as if, no one could ever understand us. But we are not abandoned if we pick up a pen or a paintbrush and write or paint. Our art will never abandon us. Our words, the pictures we draw or paint will never abandon us.

Abandonment is a state of mind, as are all other things. Let it out, so you can release it. Creative expression is the absolute best cure for addictions. If you learn to express yourself through song, dance, writing, composing, drawing or painting among other things; you will not need or even want alcohol or drugs after awhile.

I wish I would've understand that authentic creative expression, can alter your life for the better. Trying to produce the next hit song makes you less than genuine.

"We are our own devils; we drive ourselves out of our Edens."

—Johann Wolfgang von Goethe

Heaven and Hell

Channeled by Michael Hutchence

There was a time I thought
the ride would never end,

One night seemingly went into the
next, and I was laughing,
do you remember me laughing?

Unbeknownst even to myself
most of the time, I was crying,

slowly and painfully dying,
I no longer recognized
the man in the mirror
with the black hair
and the aging, puffy face

My soul was in a steady
stream of decay, for I was
not fulfilling who I was,
or why I was here on earth

Why was I on earth?
To be a self-centered,
a rock star looking for the
next party?

I was on earth to be
the light bringer...
I was on earth to be a part
of something bigger than

that which I understood
I was on earth for all of you,

Sorry, so sorry I let you down...
I'm here now, my light is shining
upon you like a huge spotlight to

bask your glory in
For you were created in heaven,
and no longer have to live in hell.

Illuminate the light you were made from,
and shine in the light I now send you
For in your light, all darkness
can and will banish and all
will come closer to God,
closer to truth and closer to love

You come from heaven,
why then do you chose to make
a living hell on earth?

"The kingdom of heaven is like a treasure hidden in a field, which someone found and hid; then in his joy he goes and sells all that he has and buys the field." (Matthew 13:4)

Michael Hutchence continues:

So one may ask, how did you Michael Hutchence, the hedonistic rock star who took his own life end up in heaven? How could that be so? My primary goal in this channeling is to share with you on earth some of what I have learned on this side. God knows your heart and intentions and every last molecule of your thought processes. You cannot hide anything from God so therefore, you should not fear God. I was not a bad person, I was misguided, at times quite self-centered but I did not seek to hurt others unless I felt personally threatened. When I returned to this side, I learned my soul was a collective of all the incarnations I had lived.

I had lived quite a few in the divine light and was quite noble and charitable. I certainly did some damage to my soul with this last incarnation as Michael Hutchence however, I did not permanently place my soul in a dangerous or exiled state away from God

I have had to work very hard on this side to evolve but please be very aware, if you consider God, the source of all intelligence and all there is, wouldn't God be the most enlightened one in existence? If enlightenment as the Buddhists teach us truly is compassion and wisdom, then do you think you will not be given ample compassion for the life you just led by the one with infinite knowledge about you and about all there is?

I did not go to hell. Oh there is a hell, just not the one you have read about. There are lower levels on this side where the very unenlightened souls go and they are positively dreadful. They create their own hell and will have to work hard to move along and come up to where I am now which is on a level very close to God.

You will feel each and everything you inflicted on everyone when you cross over, the good, the bad and everything in between. You have no idea how serious this is or what it will be like to watch your life and feel how you made others feel throughout it.

I can only tell you now; you are still on earth and have the opportunity to turn this whole thing around.

For the kingdom is inside you and you bring people closer to the kingdom. Your soul contains the hidden treasures that can bring light, love and for all intensive purposes —God, to the many you know and touch.

If I were on earth today, I would be a Buddhist who studies the Kabbalah. One area of spirituality I discussed on earth was Taoism— with two people who were quite close to me, and they will recall it. The philosophy of Taoism is something I assimilate with quite naturally. If I could have only lived in what it termed in Taoism as "WU WEI", I am quite confident I would have prevented the hell I created for myself in the last years of my human existence. When one is living in effortless action and the tenants of "WU WEI", then you are in state that aligns with God just as the rotation of the planets or the growth of a tree. You are closer to heaven when they are like this.

One of our grandest dilemma's has always been knowing when to act and knowing when not to act. If we are living in "WU WEI" then there will be no debate in our minds. It is a state that aligns all of us closer to the companionship of God we left when we came to earth but can so easily return to, effortlessly, with just our pure desire.

Two great men to study in relation to "WU WEI" are in fact, Winston Churchill and

Gandhi. A male counterpart of mine on earth has in fact been reading a fascinating book about both of these men called "*Gandhi & Churchill: The Epic Rivalry that Destroyed an Empire and Forged Our Age*" by Arthur Herman.

It is quite a well researched book and clearly illustrates action versus effortless action. I found it quite interesting my old friend selected this book. It was effortless action on his part, for he was guided to it.

As those on earth scatter around looking for the secret or the answers to "*The Da Vinci Code*" or if the Shroud of Turin is authentic, the hidden treasure is within you. As you can through the understanding of mysticism, communicate directly with God, and open those treasures within. I realize how new age it sounds to suggest, all the answers are within you, but they are. The empowerment you can achieve by believing this will astound you.

To obtain the hidden treasures of heaven within you, it's true, your views on the worldly things, the possessions, and the superficiality of it all, will be sacrificed. You will not have the time or inclination for such things. I had the most beautiful light inside of me, and I was not at all stupid, not as learned as I should've been but I certainly was knowledgeable enough to pursue a serious, inner spiritual quest. I did it in a very minute way and I regret this. The mysteries of what lies around you are nothing compared to what lies within you. Your soul is complicated, and has had a long history.

Hermetic magick and the Emerald tablets of Thoth teach us, *as is above, so is below.* It's the microcosm to the macrocosm essentially; all things have an effect on all there is. Heaven as you call it, is much like earth. There are neighborhoods on earth that are dirty, gritty and dark, and that is the same with heaven. There are beautiful neighborhoods that are well kept, happy, safe and full of light, and that is very much the same here. No one has to stay in a neighborhood that does not agree with him or her, as they can move up or move out but you must want something enough to focus on it and manifest it.

Clarify and strengthen the kingdom of your soul and when you return here, it will have been worth and all earthly sacrifice.

The Gnostic Gospel of Thomas states:

Tho 3 - "Jesus said: If those who lead you say unto you: Behold, the Kingdom is in heaven, then the birds of the heaven will be before you. If they say unto you: It is in the sea, then the fish will be before you. But the Kingdom is within you, and it is outside of you. When you know yourselves, then shall you be known, and you shall know that you are the sons of the living Father. But if ye do not know yourselves, then you are in poverty, and you are poverty"

Birthday Party

Channeled from Michael Hutchence

You've opened up your birthday presents,
and your cute, funny generic greeting cards,
but you didn't open my gift, maybe because,
it's nothing you can see

My love and light
are surrounding you now,
but fear of the intangible
makes you not want to accept
this gift, as you keep yourself in hiding

You might as well come
out in the open, for you've
only managed to obscure your path,
and despite the overgrown
trees with poisonous berries that
are surrounded by diseased embedded weeds,
your path is still there....
it's still there

As you slowly put one foot
in front of the other,
even though you believe it's
such a small gesture that it's
essentially meaningless, you
are actually manifesting the truth –
your truth

Someone gave you a sweater,
another gave a you a
shiny silver bracelet,
you can wear them now,
but you will wear
your truth forever

What you leave behind
is not a trust fund,
a secret safety deposit box,
or photos made to build a
shrine of you....

You will leave behind
your love and light,
Your greatest legacy
will be your example by
which will inspire others
to take one small step
on a path they can hardly
see, but deep down inside -
know it exists

For you are the divine magician my darling,
the Alchemist, and those around
you shall recall your ability
to manifest beauty and light
for you will have shown others
the true face of God.

On this side, it's impossible not to believe in and acknowledge the existence of Angels. There are so many celestial beings surrounding you now on earth, including Angels that you would find it nearly impossible to count them. Angels are ethereal creatures and they are not around you to interfere but to assist you with the pure love and light of God and they are from what is called, the Divine Realm—which is where there is truly one harmonic with God or what we refer to as the source. Most of us aspire to live in that realm, as the beauty and joy of it is nothing known to any of us where we are now and certainly not when we were on earth.

There are millions on earth who know believe in Angels in some form. All of the so-called mainstream religions acknowledge the existence of Angels and when it comes to Archangels, it's very interesting that each major religion believes in the existence of certain ones but does not acknowledge some of those Archangels spoken of in other religions. It's true, Angels do have a pecking order so to speak and Archangels are in fact the highest form.

I am not here to counteract anyone's religious beliefs or predispositions about Angels or Angelic realms. I am here however, to speak of my own personal experience on this side. I have been involved in a great deal of learning and spiritual work to evolve and gain an understanding of my past life as Michael Hutchence. I have worked diligently in accordance with an Archangel known on earth as Archangel Azrael.

He is a well-known figure in Muslim and Islamic traditions but I am here to tell you, regardless of your prior religious indoctrinations, he is very, very real. He is sometimes referred to as "The Angel of death" and this sounds rather ominous to many of you.

Azrael is a rather as you would say on earth, a larger than life figure but he, like all Angels tends to have varied appearances. Angels come to you in the form that they believe you will most accept or will be most likely to catch your attention. They do not have a gender so to speak and this is precisely why, an Archangel such as Gabriel may appear to some of you as a male, others as a female.

Azrael is one of the those Archangels I have yet to see appear in a female form. I have only witnessed him appear in a masculine, male form. Azrael is the Angel of transition and as I like to call him, the Angel of Ascension!

He is a predominant Archangel in helping humans cross over to this side and he has a whole band of Angels that assist him. Many of us souls on this side also do this work, and I have been involved in helping others cross over since the earth year 2002. Azrael has been my primary teacher and I have worked hard to help those in accidents (primarily motorcycle accidents) as I was a huge motorcycle enthusiast on earth, to exit their human bodies before the impact of the physical pain can be felt. This is work I take great pride in.

Azrael is the keeper of the Akashic records. There are other Archangels and celestial beings who work in conjunction with these records but the Akashic records are actually, your personal scrapbook, with all your important dates and information contained within. Azrael keeps your records, with tremendous help of course and in truth, he was one of the first Archangels ever in existence. He is also often referred to as "Ishmael."

Crossing over can be a beautiful time or it can be a confusing and difficult time. It often depends on how you led your earth life and how it came to a conclusion. Azrael is one of the greatest teachers I could ever have. When you are in this transitioned state, you will see the aspects of the earth you never knew existed and the aspects of all the dimensions you can absorb.

Azrael's goal is to help you through this transition and return you to your soul's place or origin and help you recover from your life so you may be returned to a state of grace; so you may be perfected in the eyes of God, the universe you reside in and in your own eyes.

I have been quite amazed at the fact that certain religions and their traditions do not acknowledge Azrael and even those in the so-called psychic industry do not attempt to communicate with him or ask him to help them develop their gifts.

Archangel Azrael is a powerful being who will aid those who are truly mediums or channels that connect to this side. I hear psychics on earth say, they have God and that's all they need. Well tell me then, why did God create Archangels? Why did he assign them to certain areas of work for those of you on earth? God gives you so many countless resources, but you insist you know it all and simply don't utilize the powerful Archangels or Ascended Masters on this side who are the greatest spiritual teachers in your universe or any universe for that matter.

Archangel Azrael will work with any true channel or medium who has the proper intentions in their spiritual work. Ego does not equate with God or spiritual work so he is less than likely to offer much to those, even with gifts who are dominated by or prone to bouts of self-serving ego. If your intentions are pure, he will help you develop your mediumship gifts beyond what any earth teacher could assist you with.

Closure in loss does not exist, co-existence does. I do understand perhaps when a gifted psychic helps to solve a murder case or find the body of a missing person so the family finally has some idea of what may have occurred to their loved one, it may help to close certain facts in the case. A human heart however, does not find closure, the grief, the loss, the pain, the memories etc., simply become a part of you as they assimilate into your being.

A client of a psychic who is in grief and is open minded to the notion of Archangels, is someone you may wish to consider speaking to about the Archangel Azrael.

He will often send dreams or other signals from the departed loved one or aid your loved one on this side to connect to the ones they left behind on earth. He can be a huge help for ANYONE connecting to the other side.

I suggest that if you want to hear from a loved one on the other side without the use of a channel or medium, Archangel Azrael can assist you. You must be careful in attempting this process, ask for protection perhaps from God or Archangel Michael to shield out anyone but for Archangel Azrael simply because, there are what can be termed lower energies all around the earth who are lurking and lie in wait to cause havoc. This is a very unfortunate truth so make sure you light a candle, get in a dark and quiet place, and humbly ask for protection from anyone but the all powerful Archangel Azrael.
Humbly ask this divine being to assist you in making contact with your loved one, and send your loved one lots of love and light and pray for his or her soul to God, Ascended Masters or Saints or the Archangel of your choice.
Archangel Azrael can also assist you or a gifted psychic or medium in the case of a missing person. While many psychics feel they directly tap into the energy of the missing to reveal if they are on this side or still on earth, this is

such a delicate science, Archangel Azrael can provide further information and further confirmations. I would most certainly consult him in the case of a missing person to truly determine if they have transitioned to their genuine home yet.

Archangel Azrael is connected to what is known as the "tree of life" found in the Kabbalah and other esoteric teachings. He is an Archangel long overlooked who should be given more attention because he can aid you in your most desperate hours.

Amplify

Channeled from Michael Hutchence

Amplify your heart's desire,
think of your deepest wishes daily,
say them out loud,
write them on a piece of paper

Place the paper on the wind,
and ask the Angels to read it

You'll be happily surprised
at what comes about
when you give your true desires
to the celestial beings of light;

Release your dreams -
you're free, you're free,

do not hold them anymore
for with that tight grip around them
they could not breathe
and foster in their own light.

It will be your dreams that return
to you for they were always truly
yours and always truly meant to be.

"Religions die when they are proved to be true. Science is the record of dead religions."

—*Oscar Wilde*

I would describe Oscar Wilde's novel "The Picture of Dorian Gray" as almost being the rock star's manifesto. It has to be in my opinion, one of the greatest novels ever written. The portrait in the book is obviously what happens to our souls as the celebrities and pseudo-celebrities look as youthful and cosmetically procured as possible. The image must be maintained while the decadence is decaying our souls. I look back at my life as Michael Hutchence and relate it quite well to Dorian Gray, and can see the character in the novel known as "Sybil" in my former lovers. I would antiquate one lover for the next. As I look as this novel I read on earth,

I can hardly believe I allowed myself to live it and yet I know with great certainty I have.

I was a great fan of Oscar Wilde and why not, he wrote the novel that most coincides with my previous life. Oscar by the way, has channeled to others from this side, and he still has much to say now that he has made his way out of the insanity of life on earth.

Who are you?

Channeled from Michael Hutchence

There is no doubt
you can't stay on earth forever
it's a temporary residence
that people try and keep you trapped in

So you leave while you are still
considered "young" and vital,
therefore you'll never grow old in their eyes

and you'll always be who you were
the day you supposedly died -
and they'll wish to recall that tragic moment

They want to remember you and
hold onto your energy - a piece of you -
a dream you once shared,
but holding on only holds the one you love back

For they are not stationary among

the stars, in fact they are living,
working, learning, evolving but
all earthly relationships end and
you cannot share their current journey

You are still a slave to a vibration unknown,
but they who left the earth are free to become
 whatever or whomever they wish,
with no restrictions, who then -
is more fortunate?

Life on earth is a precious gift but
a small, small part of who we are,
What is so hard to understand about this?

All is well, even if it doesn't end well,
we the free spirits go on, we are not limited,
so I would advise that you stop
being limited in how you see those
you call the dead

As you walk through the supposed
corridor of death, you learn to breathe
for the first time, you've been living
in a contained space, now you're free
and your soul rejoices in its' natural habitat

Think about the fear you have
about returning to your place of origin,
and how you try to prolong the inevitable,
because without the containment of the body,
WHO ARE YOU?

CHAPTER 4

Walk with Me and Find your Truth

"For it is a land of illusion, a place in the mind, a shimmering mirage of riches and mystery and death. These illusions have distorted its landscape and contorted its history."

—*Richard E. Lingenfelter*

Michael Hutchence:

Another teacher I have on this side I actually share the same birthday with, January 22nd. His name is Lord Byron and his major contribution to the world has been quite overlooked.

It is not often many people discuss the great poet Lord Byron in the same sentence as the Bible but he should be, after all, he was given divine information about it. The famous poet Lord Byron maybe best known as responsible for stories such as "Don Juan" and other artistic endeavors in romanticism, however, it's his work with the Holy Bible that should be very significant in his adventurous and somewhat exciting life.

As scholars now describe Lord Byron, as this extravagant, almost eccentric, flamboyant character, sounds almost as if, one is describing me in my past life as Michael Hutchence. The attributes ascribed to Lord Byron were utilized by writers in the 19th century in the creation of the "Byronic Hero." Almost every artist I have ever known seems to encompass many if not most of the characteristics that describe the "Byronic Hero." The talent in the so-called "Byronic Hero" is quite easily recognized. The passion the "Byronic Hero" exhibits seems over the top but is also quite hypnotic to those who are in his presence. The "Byronic Hero" often questions and disagrees strongly with authority and societal constraints. They are often seen as rebels and are often thought of has having, quite an ego. Most of the so-called "Byronic Heroes" actually tend to have this self-destructive streak. Is this really a good description of a "Byronic Hero" or of an artist who is highly sensitive, talented and full of moods and emotions? I would go as far to say, I was indeed what you could consider a "Byronic Hero" as were most of my comrades who was also famous for their artistic abilities on earth, such as those who were famous singers on earth who are now abiding here on this side.

Lord Byron was a deep feeling artist, and yes, like most of us, experienced his own personal demons and controversies heightened by gossip. The thing that Lord Byron needed to do the most is something I needed to do the most on earth, and that is, to be authentic to who you are. Your writing must reflect the inner you, not to be written for the purposes of what society thinks, a critic thinks or for monetary gain. Lord Byron was much more true to himself than most of us artists often were and yet, he still felt at times he had to play a role or be someone he truly wasn't. He had inner demons that often kept him from being connected to the divine realm and to God. At one point however, he was given divine direction and he followed it.

In 1816, Lord Byron was directed to go to Venice and he visited a place called Saint Lazarus Island. He became introduced to an order of Monks known as the Mechitarist Order,

and Lord Byron learned the Armenian language quite well in his time studying with the monks who were an Ancient sect; formed in the early 1700's and known for their publications of both Armenian and Ancient Greek texts.
During his studies, Lord Byron made some discoveries he was divinely guided to about the Holy Bible. He discovered some of the translations of the Bible to English were not correct or were in fact missing a few words or sentences from the Armenian version. He became particularly fascinated with the story of "Cain" from the Bible. While Lord Byron was a great inspiration to many Armenian writers, his work including his interpretation of an epistle from Paul seemed to give fear to many of the higher ups of the Catholic Church at the time.
Lord Byron felt he was a better Christian than others because he absolutely studied the Armenian language relentlessly and poured over the English version of the Bible without getting paid or being thanked or acknowledged for it. He was divinely inspired to do so and for once, he was following his inner compass that connected him right to the divine on the other side. It is true, he received divine inspiration at times for his works and channeling, but this time, an inner fire was lit and he was driven like a mad man to learn the truth of the translation of the Bible.

    Lord Byron did not discover the discrepancies in the Bible to condemn the work or make light or less of the Holy Bible. He discovered them so he could share with those reading the English Bible to be careful and somewhat cautious, as there is much lost in translation. There is always something more to what you initially see, isn't there? When you are in a state of complete acceptance without questioning or searching, your soul is not learning or evolving as it should.

There are many myths surrounding the life of Lord Byron and like most artists I have known, separating fact from fiction is quite a chore. It is true, Lord Byron was present when Mary Shelly authored "Frankenstein" and I could go into the amazing implications the novel "Frankenstein" has on the world today which is far beyond the monster films it has become (I actually portrayed Mary's husband in the film "Frankenstein Unbound") but instead I wish to say, while you may remember or even chose to discover some of the beautiful poetry Lord Byron is famous for: it is in fact his studies related to the Monks of Saint Lazarus, his grasp of the Armenian language and his findings of the faulty translations of the Bible from Armenian to English he should most be remembered and appreciated for. For the Bible is certainly worth pouring hours over and working diligently and painstakingly to find the precise interpretations, isn't it?

I now study the true version of the Bible with Lord Byron. It's hard to even begin to detail what you are missing on earth but I suggest you

Walk with Me and Find Your Truth 117

ask for God or Jesus to show you, and begin to question and study, as so many pieces will suddenly fall together for you. It is a spiritual quest most certainly worth your time and effort.

As Lord Byron said:
"Adversity is the first path to truth."

Evil

Channeled from Michael Hutchence

What is black magic? Voodoo? The occult?
What are you so afraid of?
An Evil spirit might rattle
the door or play with your lights?

The real evil you should fear
is closer than you think,
walking around on earth,
encased in human bodies,
disguising themselves as people of God

They could be the caretakers
or role models of your children,
sometimes your significant other,
you know, the one you
make excuses for (he's normal
but for when he drinks or
She's a good Mother when
She's not leaving the kids

to go out and party for two days)
Why is it you justify things
that have no justification?

Because Evil is full of excuses,
Because Evil is full of disguises
Your neighbors don't have to put
on a black robe and worship Satan
to be evil, it's all in how they
verbally abuse their children
and each other, three days out of five

Evil is so predominant
on earth at this stage
you no longer recognize it.

Look, there goes that woman
down the street, She's a witch,
She says she can see the future
and she says things are going to
happen before they actually do,
She's evil...

Maybe she can see that the man
who sleeps next to you
is really evil and you justify
his outlandish behavior everyday

Evil lurks in the hearts of all
humans, in your teenage
daughter who puts another girl
down to make her cry and loathe
herself so your little Princess can feel powerful

Evil lurks in the heart of your teenage
son who sends degrading words
to a girl online, calling her a fat slut
to send her off into a depressive
state and so she doesn't
wish to eat anymore

Do you recognize the evil in your
own home or in your own heart?

"I only did it once" is a great
justification to make you feel better
but evil always begins with a thought -
prior to an action; How many evil
thoughts do you need to engage
in the act?

The true definition of evil is,
words or actions that harm
yourself or others. Evil is
selfish and all men, women
and children have the propensity
for it; Without God in your life
and your heart, Evil may creep
through all you are and rule the
day.

A woman may say
"he's not that bad,
he's not a child molester"
But doesn't he often
molest you verbally in front

of your children?
Doesn't he molest their
tender minds with his
humiliating words when
he's had one too many?

Do you have the first
notion of what molestation is?
No one ever has to lay
a hand on you to molest you,
the assault can be done
emotionally.

Do you know what evil is?
Have you seen it?
Is it in your heart?
In your home?

Love yourself enough
to ask God to remove it,
and one way or another
your prayer will be answered.

"The world is a dangerous place to live, not because of the people who are evil, but because of the people who don't do anything about it."

—Lord Byron

CHAPTER 5

A New Dimension

"It seemed to be a necessary ritual that he should prepare himself for sleep by meditating under the solemnity of the night sky... a mysterious transaction between the infinity of the soul and the infinity of the universe."

—*Victor Hugo*

Michael Hutchence:

One of the many teachers I have learned a great deal from on this side I will refer to as Jeremy. I will now ask this great Ascended Master to enter and speak of some of the wondrous teachings he has bestowed upon me.

Channel's Note: A youthful looking man enters, with short brown curly hair and brown eyes. He is dressed in a white robe with a symbol on a shield he wears around his neck. The symbol is that of "Metatron's Cube." I am informed. I give you the exact words given to me by Jeremy, a teacher of Michael Hutchence on the other side:

"I greet you now as I am Jeremy of the 7th ray. I come forth to express to each of you, that regardless of faith or belief system, you will have what is known as a "life review" when you return to the place of your origin. You will view and feel your life as you cannot possibly do so on earth. To come out of self and see the effects, some positive, some negative, some profoundly healing, others quite hurtful that you have had on people will reshape you.

On your time scale, the life review will go by relatively quickly for the years you have spent on earth. An entire life can be viewed and experienced from different perspectives in under three hours linear earth time. It allows your soul to reach a new plateau as you realize how purposeful your life really was to many you never realized existed or were in fact effected by your thoughts and actions. The life review can be termed as bittersweet but I suggest you make changes now, and stop rationalizing that you are only on earth to care for yourself, your family and close friends. You are on earth to be of service to all you are connected to, which is all there is. You are not a piece disconnected from the puzzle or an island unto yourself and your few loved ones.

Wives often live their lives for their husbands and children. You have many husbands you may not be presently aware of. They are the men who don't have food to eat or clothes on their back. You have not taken vows to them and yet, they belong to you as you belong to others when you are in need. You have many children you did not give birth to. They include the little ones with no food to eat when they wake in the morning, no clean clothes to wear, and no one to read to them at night and make them feel safe and loved. They are your children to because you have chosen to come to earth and be a part of the human society at this time.

You are a part of the whole, not your own vehicle operating independently, devoid of reason. There is always time to give to others. It is time some of you now spend on yourself. Come out of your ego, your own little world and see the many you could personally help day in, day out and realize you cannot become a humanitarian when you have returned to heaven.

By becoming more aware of the needs of others and feeling their pain, you can begin to heal their pain. In doing so, you will heal yourself and your soul will experience a new plateau before you arrive to this destination. Many on earth have no one to wake-up next to and feel their arms around and be told, everything will be alright. Perhaps you can be that person for those who need the human touch. The emotionally battered and bruised walk among you everyday and see no compassion. Offer compassion, offer your heart, it will not return broken. But you say, you must support your family. Your family is all around you, it's each person you come into contact with everyday, as you may regard them as strangers, but you will come to see when you return to heaven, there are no strangers in heaven as there are no strangers on earth.

Assumptions are made by many of you daily about different people and their respective feelings. You will find that many of your assumptions, if not most were quite inaccurate in many cases when you undergo your life review. By then it is too late to change the course of events. I suggest dismissing assumptions about those around you. It will make your actions of a much more pure state of being. All human beings have suffered from rejection and states of feeling unloved, and another human being could have easily helped to lift that state you were in along with the pain that accompanied such torment. Lift the pain of as many as you can while on earth, they are your family, you are supporting them."

"Love is composed of a single soul inhabiting two bodies."

—Aristotle

Channel's note: Jim Morrison returns and introduces me to a female spirit, I can hear a sweet voice but only see a large blob of purple energy with an intense magenta colored energy within. Jim informs me she is what is known as an "Elemental" and when I ask him what it is, he simply explains her as a "nature spirit." He proceeds to tell me, Elementals are not as predominant as Angels but they are Ancient Spirits that many who walked the earth were aware of and in communication with.

Jim also references something known as "Lords of the Watchtower" and he asks me to take down each word of the conversation he is about to have with a spirit only known to me as an "Elemental."

Jim: Where have they taken my jewels? They were for her, my true love, she's still on earth. I need to have them ready for her when she comes home. I need to give her sapphires, rubies, emeralds and of course, diamonds.

Elemental: You do not need to give her jewels. She will recognize you, for you are her jewels James. The promise of your love, the promise of eternity with you, will indeed be her treasures.

Jim: But I must greet her with gifts!!! I must show her I am her betrothed.

Elemental: You have lost the ability to give her earthly possessions.

Jim: But why? I have nothing to give her then, all I would be able to give her is...me. It won't be enough; I was supposed to be with her on earth. I was supposed to give her this beautiful life; she has struggled so much without me.

Elemental: James, your Rebecca will simply want you and your love, not the material things you would have provided her on earth. Did you truly love those that you gave material things to on earth?

Jim: I was not in love with any of them and they never captivated my soul.

Elemental: There is your answer, she has your soul, and that will mean more to her than the things of earth that fade away. Material gifts on earth are considered disposable; your soul and love are eternal James.

Jim: I want to be able to make up to her what I wasn't there to give her now. I can hardly wait for her. I've waited so long.

Elemental: Is she not worth the wait?

Jim: Yes, yes she is but I'm basically in a state of limbo or worse. I can't be free with her and you know that. Would you help me prepare for her?

Elemental: I bring you the news you've waited for James. Your butterfly comes to you soon. This pain you are in James is not in vain. The way you live for her on this side is one of the most beautiful things we can behold. Your vigil will bring her to you. Her soul now hears yours and will soon wish to be reunited.

(There is no response from Jim for a few minutes)

Elemental: James, did you clearly understand what I just communicated to you?

(I view Jim moving around crazily)

Jim: I am relieved, very, very happy. This has been like being thirsty on earth, with no water ever available to me. Thank you Elemental, I must go and prepare for her now.

Elemental: You are manifesting her soul coming to yours like a powerful magnet. You draw her closer each earth day James. Do not lose faith.

Jim: I can't, I won't. She is all I ever wanted. She is all I ever need. She is all there is to me — my jewels.

CHAPTER 6

Poet's Lament

"Poetry is nearer to the truth than oral history."

—*Plato (from Ion)*

Room 32

Channeled from Jim Morrison

Come to my room,
don't knock too loudly,
it's just like the one
I occupied on earth
with the number "32"
on the door

It's rather ironic I can travel
anywhere in the universe,
but I have chosen to lock
myself in this small,
dingy room in the color
green some would
describe as sickly

I keep myself contained
though I can go to any
dimension of this universe
or the next because I have
no wanderlust, no fortitude,
until my woman returns home

I have built her a house
that I rarely enter,
as I am filled intense
longing and sadness,

I must wait to show her
this temple I erected in her name
So I sulk in this room,
confine myself from the light,
and compose love letters
and poems exclusively to her

I think of the time,
I would've had on earth with her
and hold onto it tightly
as a Buddhist monk
strokes his prayer beads,

I paw at what would've been,
and what will be
I think of her without me,
and I sink so low, and realize
my whole entire past existence
had one goal, to reach her and it
remains my only option

When I somehow slithered
through the pearly gates,

I wanted to be the greatest
universal voyeur,
the greatest student and
hence, a respected teacher,
to contact all my earthly
idols and penetrate deeply
their layers of wisdom,

to become the enlightened
ambassador of this universe
or the next...

I wish to travel beyond the
containment of this room,
past Venus to become
a pioneer of what I could
only imagine on earth,

but I cannot do this now,
until she returns, until
she comes to me, I cannot
do anything without her, it would
be meaningless in ways unforeseen
by the stars...

My room, this room,
looks like it did on earth,
lumpy mattress, unkept,
until a kind maid wonders in,

though I do not smoke here,
I do not drink, I don't have
groupies showing up at all
hours, I have no one night stands,

I have no company, I sulk, I dream,
I regret, I wait, I write....

If only I had known on earth,
I would not get past this old

motel room, I would've stuck
around and waited for her,

but I bask in this poet's lament until
She returns, and I'll never step foot
in room 32 again...

Jim Morrison: If I had to come back to earth and chose any sort of incarnation through time, I would in fact select the lifetime of a scribe in the Mesopotamia. It was a time when cuneiform writing was the most interesting thing to do and one would never really be subjected to writer's block. I would live back thousands of years ago, and I am not suggesting I didn't live long ago, but the life as a scribe in the Mesopotamia would be my clear choice. The Mesopotamia is the cradle of civilization and I believe, what that region of the earth now symbolizes between Iraq, parts of Iran and Syria is a clear indicator in the direction civilization has gone and these war torn regions of hate, are clearly a sad, sad statement of what has propelled a divisive downfall of the natural energy harmonic of the planet.

I of course, would entertain no possibility of any incarnation minus my beautiful, eternal soul mate. I would not consider ever being separated from her again and it may surprise many, but in my last incarnation as the Lizard King (Boo, hiss), I only appeared in that lifetime to have an earth life with her. It would've been our greatest existence together and yet, I couldn't make it through that life without her. I left the earth without having had the chance of meeting her, let alone giving her the life I had promised her on the other side. If I had to do over again, I would not have lived that life or incarnated as James Douglas Morrison. It's damaging to the soul to experience such a turbulent and unfocused incarnation. I would be happier as a scribe, in ancient times, exploring the stars and the sky in ways that had never been written about before, with my eternal soul mate by my side, in a simple, uncluttered existence.

Lost Winter
Channeled from Jim Morrison

I walked by and saw the two of you,
little girls laughing and making snow angels,
uninhibited by the rotted soil
underneath the glacier like layers
you laid in...

By some strange lack of discernment,
a dark force came upon you and entered
your most sacred chamber and stole your light,
I am here to tell you, that I have retrieved it for you...

It's contained in a white box with a red ribbon,
and you will find it stored on the highest shelf
in the closet in the bedroom upstairs,
first door on the left in the house of Avalon...

I fought the dark forces to regain your light
until ....there was nothing left of me,
for as I strolled past you in that wintertime
of so long ago, innocently making a snow
angel, I kept walking....

Your angelic presence and
ecclesiastical grace was something
instinctively...I was not worthy of..
so I have spent many full moons becoming
the Avenger to return what is rightfully yours...

The pseudo vampires took my very soul
so I could return yours....they believed
they were ancient predators and to win
their acclaim and gain their rituals of magic,
I had to join their circle of emptiness corrupted
by their false understanding of their ancestors
so long ago...

I will take you to the box...your box...
and then ask you...Am I now worthy of
you?

Can I bask in your light on a fiercely cold
winter's night? Will you shield me from
the wind....take me as your lover....
as you will reclaim your wings as the Angel

oblivious to the rotted soil that lies below
and I will no longer have to walk past you.

Waiting for the Spring
Channeled from Jim Morrison

My wild love has gone
and left me alone
in a cauldron of pain...
Her ship came in,
it was in the form of another
lover and she sails the
Caribbean and to parts unknown,
as I stew in my cauldron of pain...

She ravishes in the sunlight,
warm beaches and tropical sunscts,
I sit in misery on a bar stool,
raging to the cynical bartender
about what a junkie the man
who lives upstairs is,
and what a shrew his old
lady is and how she gives
good head...

Oh yes, she gives great head
but she's not as good as my
wild love, my beautiful, blonde Angel
with those big bountiful breasts

sweet lips and gifted tongue,
She looks like a stripper but she is
my true intellectual match...
I have read the novels and I shall
quote the prose, my wild love has
read the non-fiction, and knows the list
of secrets and secret lovers each of you
keeps...

She has intuition, she's a mystic of old,
so I must do all I can, with all my might
to bring her back home...

Who else can look me in the eye
and get a straight answer, without
the silly game of seeing what I can
get away with?

I'm tired of missing her, longing for her kiss,
I have no real ambition mind you,
I have but one desire...

Bring my girl home, tell my woman
I need her here now, She is like a wild colt,
no one can break or control,
and I am like a Shaman who is unaware
how to rouse the dead or use
my vast cures seen only
in the furthest reaching
ceremonies that fail
to invoke the light....

I've waited for the Spring for
too long, my crazy woman
ran off with some guy because
She gives great head
and she doesn't realize
he doesn't care about much
past that - for men can live
on head and sex forever....

So he has her in his bed while
visions of revenge swirl loudly
in my soon to be numbed head,
BUT WAIT, maybe

She'll dump him and return
once more to her room and
She'll call me to see her and I'll
stop over and talk about why
she left me, and maybe I'll finally
understand why waiting for the Spring
was worth it - for She'll return in May
and I'll show up in time to say "Stay
with me Rebecca, among the ruins,
we will find treasure" and I will hold
her face in my hands and tell her

"You are the Springtime, the seasons
only change because of you."
May is a long way off but I will
wait for the Spring, it's all I have -
She's all I ever want to know.

Indigo Summer

Channeled from Jim Morrison

I tell myself, the answers lie in the Canterbury
Tales, if Chaucer would have completed them.
Each traveler telling two tales on their journey—
those unwritten tales unlock the secret code
I need to make this happen.

I must return to my own tales, just as the
Canterbury Tales—they were never completed,
come back to earth and bring her home,
She is my holy shrine in Canterbury,
my final destination.

Indigo Bride, I must come for you
in the heart of the Indigo Summer.
The haze of the moonlight
fills the trees as I wait for her
to emerge from her rose covered bath.

I don't know when She became my obsession,
for I recall nothing before her.
I am the intrepid voyeur for each move
she makes never fails to excite and provoke me.

The time has come,
I have waited for this Summer since 1943?
Is this a cosmic joke??
My Indigo Bride, can't you see
an Indigo Bunting looks at you

from the tree near your bedroom window.

As you stare at this beautiful
specimen of nature's true romance,
I will appear to bring you home once and for all.

For I am your home and I can't
live without you, as we are nature's
true testament to Indigo love.

The Mysteries of Autumn
Channeled from Jim Morrison

As I sat in Paris in Springtime,
I dreamt of Autumn in New York,

for in New York, all four seasons
could be felt and seen as they should be...

The Magic of the changing leaves
under the harvest moon was a
dream; I cannot go back to
New York in Autumn
until my true loves accompanies me.

She remains a great mystery
as to how and where, but She's
finally scheduled to arrive home
in time to watch the leaves change

in New York, and to hold my hand
as we glide under the harvest
moon.

New York City always called
my name. I loved the excitement,
the people, bookstores, the bars,
the delis, the energy of it all, but now
I can share the energy and above
all the mysteries of Autumn in
New York City with my one,
true love.

She will love what I love
and see things through my eyes
for the first time this year....

Nothing can divide true love,
Nothing can stop us now....

Jim Morrison continues:

If I were still on the earth, there are a few places I would love to dearly be. Of all the great museums in the world, it would be the British Museum in London I would spend most of my time in. I cannot tell you the gift you have in this museum, but it's a place I could go for many days at a time and never grow bored or tired. Whether it's the temple of Athena or the artifacts from the Mesopotamia that intrigue me the most, it's hard to say. The Rosetta Stone is there, I can pretty much tell each and everyone of you, the answers to the world yesterday, today and tomorrow lie in this building. There are the most incredible ancient documents housed in this building and each of them is far more valuable than any monetary amount can foretell. I am sorry they have closed the round reading room. I would have liked to have passed away in that room if I were still on earth.

I would actually have homes in a few places on the globe with my wife and one place I could truly see myself spending lots of time, would be Lake Como, the jewel-like oasis in Italy. The architecture, the tranquility, the ambience, and the weather would all agree with me. I would want to spend many months in Lake Como and also in New York City. There is no doubt, I would no longer be a resident of L.A. but may have had a place further north in California, in wine country.

I have always had a true fondness for New York, and my wife and I would often take in the theater there. I would say New York would've surely become my home base. I would do extensive traveling and those would include trips to Egypt. I would like to have explored the Middle East through the years and continue to travel around America, probably to small towns, with diners and engage in conversations with what every day folks, which were always the people I best related to and enjoyed studying. I would not be alone, once I met my wife, I would not let her out of my site for the most part.

    I think at times, she may have found it overwhelming and I think that even now, when she feels my passion and love for her when she comes to this side, she may very well find me to be too much. But that won't stop me for trying. You can have access to all the beauty in the world, the riches, the women, every luxury but in the absence of true love, it's all for nothing.

Teardrops
Channeled from Jim Morrison

Do not feel alone Rebecca,
as I will never leave you,
you possess my soul
as only you can,
and I'm not going
anywhere without you
holding my hand

You don't have to dream
about the joy I will bring to you
my love, I will make you quickly
forget all your earthly pain,

You are the spark that will ignite
our eternal flame
Your tears combined with mine
will be placed in the ocean;

We will not know of them again,
Cry no more, this is our beginning
and I promise you, we shall have no end.

The fire they will see from earth
is not just me, it's you and me Rebecca,
twin flames, melded into one,
it will all be for us honey,
our time will soon come

Return to the Sea
Channeled from Jim Morrison

I long to find the mermaid
of my dreams...with the long
golden hair and the face of an
Angel...I have never been
able to catch-her

The monarch Chrysalis of
that enchanted creature swimming
in the sea...for she is free...
and I could swim with her for all eternity...

I long to swim under the ocean...
and go deep, deeper to find
the pearl troca shell I have seen
in my sweetest dreams..
for when I uncover it....hidden in the waves

of my nocturnal haze...a vibrant purple
and a misty teal emerge and cover me...
and I see her swimming by....
I will follow her...I must stroke her

She is not a sea creature...
She is my creature...
She does not speak...
She softly kisses me...
I am a sailor of old
and she is Rebecca...
my dream, my wife...
my eternal haven

CHAPTER 7

The Dark Stars

"I do not like the men on this spaceship - They are uncouth and fail to appreciate my better qualities."

—*quote from the movie "Dark Star"*

Jim Morrison:

Once on earth, in one of my many infamous notebooks, I wrote the words "you don't call, you don't write, do your orgasms still belong to me?" Who were those words written for? No one I knew. I just wrote down random thoughts and mainly those words were from women I knew about how I didn't pay them enough attention to them since I was really awful at trying to maintain relationships.

I was, rather dark and disturbing around many people but now, I have taken a new path. It's a lonely and hard waiting for my mate, but I have evolved and will continue to do so. Not everyone on this side evolves however, it's free will. I have met those more evolved than I am of course and plenty that are not. I have never met anyone over here like John Simon Ritchie (you know him as Sid Vicious). It's not that he doesn't want to evolve exactly, but I am starting to believe, he is comfortable basking in his own glory. We have agreed to include him in the book, for a variety of reasons. Namely to demonstrate the various levels we are all on in this dimension and time is not a concept that matters. Meaning, Michael Hutchence who showed up in 1997, is more evolved than I am and many others. I have limited myself to completing things until my true love comes home. Just because Sid came here long before Michael Hutchence means nothing. I will say, he has come along way because previously Sid didn't believe in God, spirit guides, angels or anything else over here, he kept to himself. Now he is opening up and has agreed to give my channel his story. I really hope Sid continues to work on things. His earth life is over. He should just let it go.

Jac = Jacqueline Murray (Channel)
SV = Sid Vicious (formerly of "The Sex Pistols")

Jac: Hello Sid. Previously you identified yourself as John to me. What would you like to be called?

SV: Anything really, not your dog, you can call me John. I was called in before, by psychics, and they can fuck off because I don't want to be seen in their crystal balls. I will only talk to you, cause you don't care about the shit all the others care about.

Jac: Thanks, I think. How do you feel about the movie made about you called "Sid & Nancy?"

SV: The movie wasn't that bad, but Gary Oldman as me; that's fuckin' stupid. It's absurd, a travesty. Gary Oldman has some strange fuckin' shit going on in his own head. If they want to make a movie about me they have to find someone who can get inside who I was. If

Amy Winehouse were male, then maybe, but she's a fuckin' mess. She's a kooky bitch who I think would be my equal and we would come to physical blows.

Jac: Would you consider the film factually accurate? Or would you like to correct anything?

SV: I was abused and mistreated throughout my life. My Mum tried very hard you know but Anne was just umm, really in a pickle as they old hags use to say. She got involved with complete assholes and they would leave us and well one died, same thing, he left. I never had a fuckin' father and if there is one thing I wish I had in my past life, it was a Dad. People think you don't need that, you can get by with a Mum and that's a complete crock of shit. I hated myself, my life and the fact I didn't really have a family but a struggling Mum who kept on struggling, didn't know how to dig herself out of the hole she got herself into. Having a dog was the best thing for me growing up. A dog loves you no matter what and every kid should have one you know, a dog, a companion and find that unconditional love he can't find in his parents.

Jac: I am sorry to hear about that John. How do you feel about the "Sex Pistols" past and present?

SV: I know others will say I am this or that, but I was the Sex Pistols and even now it seems punk music is most strongly identified with me. This is why Malcolm put me in the group you see. They wanted to be something; I was something. They acted their roles and I lived it. I was the only Sex Pistol who lived it while the others faked it. I was real to what the band was, and at some stage it all went bloody mad because you see the jealousy. Johnny Lydon can piss off as much now as he could then. He was the one who drove me from the band. He was the one who couldn't stand that everyone knew that Sid Vicious was the Sex Pistols and still is. No one looks at him and thinks anything about him other than when he was in the band with me. I wasn't a clever guitarist. I was the identity of the entire band and later came to identify the entire punk movement.

I wanted to spit on Johnny and the others who didn't want to accept the award at the Rock N' Roll Hall of fame because that was my award. Without me and the legend of me, who'd care about the lot of them?

People want to know what happened to me and how it all went down. I was abused as a kid, really abused. Things my Mum never knew about. I was basically wrecked before I turned 15. I'm still angry like I was on earth. I am just glad not to be in that piss hole anymore. But at least give me my due. I am only asking to be thought of as the identity of punk music because I lived the anarchy and chaos more so than others that just dressed the part.

Jac: So after all this time, isn't all water under the bridge?

SV: No and it never will be. They can piss off.

Jac: Would you like to talk about Nancy now?

SV: I think I should talk about Nancy now. Not the best subject for me but everyone wants to know about us, and I see Nancy you know. I see her and have seen her but we aren't a couple. We weren't lovers like lovers should be. We were fucked up lovers and she got me hooked on that putrid shit and that's why we can't be together now. She took me into her world when I should've lived in my own world. She was like a bad case of the clap really. It's fun when you get it but it burns and burns. I have gotten to see our life when I went to this side and I see her calling the shots and I fucking hate it. If I wasn't so fucked up I would have told her to piss off. She was a dreadful bore after awhile and I loved her because she kept putting the needle in my vein. I loved her because I was so ill with hepatitis and other shit; I had no one else who gave a fuck if I slept in an alley.

Now I'll talk about Karma. Nancy and I think we will find a way to rid ourselves of it because I do not want to continue with her. They would say she had problems and was troubled and that's because no one ever really fuckin' understood her or loved her. I wanted to love her. Love just doesn't bloody work when you are sticking that putrid shit in your veins. You can't even fuck. You can't do much of anything but piss yourself. I was someone else before Nancy came along. I tried that putrid shit before I met her but it made me puke endlessly in a toilet so I didn't want it after that. You couldn't have Nancy without that putrid shit so I took it all. But in doing so, I lost my identity. I didn't know who I was after awhile. I know now and I am not the person you see with Nancy. I was the identity of the Sex Pistols and the punk movement as you call it before I met her. I lost that with her. I lost myself. I lost it all.

Jac: John, that seems rather harsh and unkind, even now. Do you want to speak about Nancy's death? Were you involved?

SV: I was so powerful in my own right at one time. I should not have gone and lost my identity to someone else. It was done with and because of the putrid shit. If I was not fucked up, I would've gotten away from her because I have replayed the events and she was a carnivore. I wasn't her first choice. She wanted a star and took my identity away. Her death was in many ways her own fault. I say this because you stinking bastards who write about it know nothing about it. As I said, she was calling the shots, and Nancy had this piss poor excuse for a parasite come over and she bought these fuckin' pills and actually put them in my mouth. I almost died three times before this night. Three times because of the putrid shit and hepatitis and the only thing anyone can see out of this was, that Nancy was trying to kill me because these pills are what you call oxymorphone and they could kill a fucking horse. She gave me so many and I was out of it. I thought I was in a knife fight I had before and I wasn't going to let this bloody bloke beat me down again like a fuckin' dog. I had no memory of killing her. I never remembered on earth but I did it. I took her life. Can anyone be held responsible for what they do on that shit? Those fucking pills or that putrid shit? I say not because you don't know what in the bloody world you are doing or who you are doing it to.

Sometimes, someone would fuck me and I wouldn't even know. I had this other girl when Nancy and I were apart who would show-up and end up in bed with me. She said we had sex and I didn't know what we did. I don't take the fall for Nancy's death. I won't be the whipping boy because if she hadn't given me those fuckin' pills, that she knew caused a person to be completely out of it, she'd be walking around probably married to some old rock star laying on his fat stomach. She continually made it so I was fucked up and I was so gone, I didn't care. I was incoherent in those days, the days when she died. I tried to take my own life because my identity was taken from me. Nancy Spungen was my identity, I was her chained dog because of that putrid shit. I was told I killed her but I couldn't remember it. I didn't know who I was after that. I had no identity anymore.

Jac: Whoa John, back up please. So you are saying you murdered Nancy but take no responsibility? I mean didn't you see what you did in your life review when you crossed over?

SV: Yes I saw it. I wish I had never done it but I can't take it back.

Jac: Are you sorry for it?

SV: I am but I'm not. Don't remember it, so what do you want me to say?

Jac: She was killed rather brutally John.

SV: Rockets Redglare should've gone to jail because he sold her the pills that night and decided he was going to rob us. Why not? We were easy to rob, and so out of it we'd never know. When Rockets came to the room later, he saw Nancy bleeding and she asked him for help. He stole a roll of money out of the drawer and took off. He could've saved her life. He killed Nancy just as much as I did. He killed my identity and while I didn't want to kill Nancy, I killed myself as I killed my identity, my entire world.

Jac: So John, do you want to clear up anything about your own death?

SV: I had no idea who I was but began to find myself again in jail, off the putrid shit. I began to be abused again and I didn't like it or who I was. I began to see, I had allowed my identity to be taken and when I got it back, it wasn't the same as it had ceased to become anything more than what was left after the remnants of that putrid shit and Nancy Spungen. I tried to live on. I tried to find my way but when you lose yourself for that long of a time, how do you find yourself? I met this girl, Michelle who I know would've been good for me because she was not the identity snatcher Nancy was. I met her and I could've gone on with her. Unfortunately my Mum, not meaning to, got me some of that putrid shit and overdosed me. I couldn't tolerate it like I did before. It was out of my system and out of my identity you could say.

My Mum is with me and we have gone over it and it's not something we talk about here. It's not important anymore because it wasn't intentional. She didn't mean to do it and I never meant to kill Nancy, what goes around comes around you could say. Nancy was more clever than people think. She knew what she was creating when she got me she had to live with the consequences. I have asked her for forgiveness because it was an awful way to go and she has given me her forgiveness because she knows her life was a mess and she really feels better off she didn't have to go on with it. Her mind was snapping in two and she didn't want to have to continue like that. Her personality was splitting you could say. She had taken my identity and could not see herself giving it back.

Jac: Ok so, is there anything else you would like to clear up about yourself? I am still fairly shocked at the lack of empathy for the murder victim and her family. Nancy did have a family John.

SV: People are curious about me, about Sid, not the other Sex Pistols. I think you should be because there was more to me than anyone ever saw or knew. I have had others try and bring me in and one time, I was reading a comic book and told them to piss off. I still like comic books (Smiles) and I think I thought about these graphic novels before they appeared. Nancy wants the world to know she forgives me and I do not take responsibility for things I did that I was not aware I was doing.

I may have taken beatings but people like David Coverdale deserved what they got when his wife was cheating on him with a real murderer who was aware what he was doing though he was coked up. He still felt what he did. I felt nothing. I felt dead because Nancy had taken my identity. How did it feel for David to know his wife was boinking O.J.? Todd Smith deserved to be cut with a beer glass, I did what I did and I stand by it.

Jac: This stuff still matters to you here and now?

SV: Yes, so just listen. I use to cut myself with a knife and I did it more so after Nancy died. I wanted to feel again. I wanted to feel who I was, what was my identity?
I make no apologies here because that isn't for those reading this. What I have to say is done here in person, onc on one. I have learned that I was born with this thing, this bi-polar thing or manic you call it. I had this brain imbalance with the chemicals running around in it and I was easy prey for someone to come and take hold of me and reshape me. I was who I was and I should not have been reshaped. I was Simon John Ritchie. I was Sly. I was John Simon Ritchie, I was Sid and I am to this very day, Sid Vicious. I am not one to go and talk to these thieves who tell your future. I don't care for them. I didn't show at the séance some bitch singer had for me. I talk to you because I like you luv. I want to reach out and touch you

because your light is really very nice. You may not know what to make of these words but you are taking them down like I give them to you.

Many young people now felt the way I did and they feel oppressed and they won't be the cheerleader. They want to have their own identity and proudly express it no matter how much shit you throw out them. Is this who you thought I was? I wasn't in a love story. My identity was snatched out from under me. I have it back now and at least you can say I never pretended to be something I wasn't. I was never a fuckin' fake. I was true to myself and true to you with no bullshit. People would say that you had to walk on the other side of the street when you saw me. Those people, knew the real me. That's all I came to say.

Jac: Thank you. I can't say this wasn't disturbing for me, but I did agree to take your words down as you gave them to me. I really hope you heal even more from your past life.

SV: Thanks luv. I feel more like me and don't want to give up my identity again. See you later.

Jim = Jim Morrison
Mic = Michael Hutchence
KC = Kurt Cobain
Jac = Jacqueline Murray (Channel)

KC: We wanted to come back in and sort of rap this up, whatever this is. It's been a really good thing for me Jacquie. Thank you for allowing me to come through.

Jac: Thank you, I think the channeling you gave me is incredibly interesting and layered.

KC: Thanks, there are many layers to it. All these people go around and write all this shit about me and make all this money and I don't really care if they make money but, I sometimes peruse what is written about me and I wonder, what the hell is the person writing that stuff thinking? I understand how Jim feels about it. We have no control over it and we aren't meant to but it's pretty lame. There is one author that wrote two books about me and also one about Jimi Hendrix that me and Jimi do like.

Jac: You gave me the name earlier, Charles.

KC: Right, Charles R. Cross. People judge him for putting out private words and now pictures of mine, but better him than others. Someone else would've put it out and his intentions are not really that bad. He wants to show the human side to me and to Jimi Hendrix. I am not crazy about any of this being done but I know someone else would've done it.

Jim: Well I hope he never writes about me. There is too much out there already, too many books, articles, reminiscing and other assorted tributes that are plain bullshit.

Jac: You really don't want to be remembered Jim, do you?

Jim: Since I no longer own that past life and have moved on, I wish everybody else would. I can give you a 1,000 or more better people right now to write about, read about and study.

Mic: Angel, I would like to interrupt and say I am very grateful once again for the opportunity you have given me to record my sentiments.

Jac: You are welcome Michael, and I thank you.

Mic: I know the channeling of Sid Vicious (John Simon Ritchie) was quite disturbing for you.

Jac: I am not here to give my opinions on what you give me. I need to emotionally detach from it, but in the case of what Sid gave me, it was incredibly intense.

Mic: How can you detach when you are also an empath and you have felt the things we have given you from the beginning?

Jac: I do but I don't want to be judgmental and I must allow all of you to give me your stories and for me not to impose my own thoughts.

KC: You never had your own thoughts about me (Smiles). You weren't a fan and didn't know more than one song I sang.

Jac: True, I also remember when you did cross over Kurt, seeing some people crying and thinking they were taking it a little far, acting like you were their next door neighbor or something. I didn't get it, and I didn't get you. I'm sorry.

KC: But now you do, I'm a lot like your next door neighbor (Smiles) and a good friend. Don't worry about not getting me. I had a hard time being understood by just about everyone.

Jim: I want you to pay attention to something about Sid, Jacquie.

Jac: Yes?

Jim: He's holding onto his human identity. He's living in the personage he was on earth.

The first key to evolving on this side is, to put your past earth existence behind you and lose that identity.

Mic: Those previous earth identities are too attached to ego. I can still be Michael but I am not Michael, the hedonistic rock star. Sid is holding onto a name that someone else gave him and this identity he created for himself and in his case, literally lived. That identity will be of no use to him in this dimension and in truth, will be a huge obstacle to his own personal evolution.

KC: When I first spoke to you, I didn't come in and say hey, I'm Kurt Cobain, I was in Nirvana. I just said "Hi, I'm Kurt, a friend of Jim's" and wanted to talk.

Jac: I had no idea who you were.

KC: I am just Kurt now and I can't tell you how nice it is just to communicate with you.

Jac: Thank you

KC: You're welcome. Those earthly identities that people want to cling to are almost amusing.

Mic: Yes, well keep in mind, when I was on earth, I made up some stories about my family members and backgrounds at times. I did so because it was about the image I wanted to create as a star, to make the story more interesting and to pepper it with intriguing but false details. At times, I began to name drop quite a bit, and when you get to that stage, I am afraid your ego has taken a very wrong turn. I would brag about the people I knew or dined with. When I was around the fashion industry due to my girlfriend at the time, I really got very caught-up in celebrity. It was an incredibly shallow thing. My point is, I created many false details about myself at times and tried to feel important because of who I rubbed shoulders with, so I would suggest many, many others do the same on earth. You aren't seeing the real person, you aren't seeing the soul, you are seeing this major mirage.

Jim: That was my point earlier Jacquie, those who sit on earth stating things like "I knew Jim Morrison—you didn't" are clearing showing their egos which need to be reconsidered.

KC: That's infuriating; they don't know us anymore, not by long shot.

Mic: What happens is, sometimes people who did love or care about you, want to clarify what they conceive as misconceptions or lies about you, but at some point, people come out of the woodwork who are essentially what I would term as "hangers on" and that's their purpose, to hang on to you and the relationship they had with you on earth. Some of them embellish it, and it's merely an attempt to attach to you or your image, via their own ego. It's certainly not healthy for them to continue to hang on to you once you have gone to the other side and besides, they will never stop what others wish to say or write about you. It simply becomes a war of words that nobody wins.

Jim: Right, and while I do like Jerry Hopkins who has written about me at nauseam, enough is enough. To examine the incidents I was involved in—the drunkenness, the descent into my own painful hole—is really purposeless. I can tell the story better than anyone else and I have done so, in our first book and anyone who chooses not to believe it, I don't have really any regard for. I would think if anyone would try to communicate from the other side, it would be me. While there are others who "claim" to channel me and who claim I am around them, in truth, look at the volume of work we have written Jacquie. What did you do, make it all up and create poetry and a story that was never in your mind?

Jac: It's rather sad for me, Jim. Your story is depressing, and if I wanted to attempt to write fiction, I would have thought you were happy and having a good time doing your own thing.

Jim: Far from it, so far from it. I wanted to have a good time, but I couldn't do so sober.

Mic: We are in another dimension now Angel, not judging those who don't believe in this type of communication because we weren't the most spiritual people when we walked the earth however, we simply need to align now with people who can accept we are communicating from this dimension. We need to give our energy to people who would be open to this. We don't condemn those who are not but look at it like beginning a new project. Those who are on board with you will get your attention and energy; those who are not will need to be left behind.

Jim: Yep. I look at earth right now and I see the information highway that so many attach to, but for those who don't have that luxury and live a simpler existence, I see these ridiculous, almost absurd redundancies of superfluous information about my former existence. Why would anyone care what I ate, what I drank, how tall I was or what I did alone for hours? Why would anyone debate this or become engaged in dialogue in this vast wasteland of strangers online? When I saw some of this junk, I could not be more disengaged from those sorts of people. I am quite disengaged with everyone from my past life and was during those final months in Paris.

Jac: So Jim, you have no affection for the internet?

Jim: I give my affection elsewhere. I realize how significant the internet is to the modification of the work of many on earth but, the sources of information on it should be scrutinized. I don't think I would even read books online Jacquie. I'd prefer a physical book I could have in my hands literally on earth. I would more than likely use email for business correspondence but would still like to pen personal letters and mail them via the good ol' U.S. Postal service because there is a loss of intimacy with email. I also wouldn't want my email to be deleted. People could always rip-up or throw away the hard copy but, there is true beauty to writing letters.

Jac: I understand Jim.

Mic: Unlike Jim, I always loved technology and gadgets.

Jim: I would however love the technology in photography and would probably spend a fortune on those types of things.

Mic: I would be texting all the time if I were on earth.

Jim: That's another place Michael and I differ, I was not one who liked the phone very much but for short conversations. I preferred in person conversations when at all possible and Michael loved talking on the phone.

Mic: Yes I did, all night.

KC: It's really kind of an interesting thing though, that Michael Hutchence was such a fan of both me and Jim.

Mic: Yes I was and still am, on a much more personal level.

KC: I was a fan of Sid's.

Jac: OH MY GOD.

KC: Yes, loved the Sex Pistols.

Jim: Kurt and I have something else in common.

KC: We sure do, certain authors who were a huge inspiration to both of us, like Jack Kerouac, and we both loved "Waiting for Godot", though nothing really happens to the characters waiting, there's a lack of action. I relate my past life to that in many ways.

Jac: Do any of you miss anything on earth? All of you seem so past it.

Mic: Our daughters.

KC: Yes our baby girls, though mine is all grown-up and Michael's is just about there, and you know that Jim misses someone on earth.

Jim: The only part of earth I miss, my darling Rebecca.

KC: After I did what I did, I instantly regretted it because of my daughter. I want her to know I am around her, and it's hard like this to be her Dad, but she has to notice things in her bedroom. I am there so often.

Mic: That is certainly what I miss on earth, raising my daughter, and Kurt and I are still with our girls but it's quite different, and we certainly would rather still be in human form for their sake's.

KC: And our own, so they didn't have to live with the fact, we left them.
If I could've come out of the pain and just taken that time and left things and people on earth like I planned, I'd be with my daughter today and hopefully had been good for her.

Mic: I would be much more spiritual and be a much better Dad today than I was. I'd be really out of my own world and make it all about Tiger. Jim is a co-dependent soul and he really needs his other half to complete him. He's in a different position. Kurt and I will wait for our girls, we will be here and they will learn how we never truly left them.

KC: They will learn how sorry we are and how we much we love them. (Kurt becomes emotional). Why do people write there are no tears in heaven? We feel, we love, we miss our kids. I mean maybe an Angel has no tears or some celestial being or something of that nature, but we do.

Jac: I am sorry. Maybe people want to believe there are no tears in heaven.

Mic: Just like they want to believe the mirage of who others claim to be, like celebrities and politicians.

KC: The one who is the hardest to live with over here is actually Jim.

Jac: I would've never guessed.

Mic: He just waits, paces and is quite angry and then very sad. It's no garden of roses being near him.

Jim: Thanks Michael.

Mic: We will be as happy as Jim is when his mate returns home. We can hardly wait.

KC: We can't, but Jacquie, I wanted to mention, the poems I gave you, have various meanings to different people.

Jac: Yes, that's interesting.

KC: The red roses and the word refuge have meanings to some I knew in various ways.

Jac: I understand Kurt, I liked both of them. They were so different.

KC: Thank you.

Jim: My mention of things has various meanings too, those who get it, good for them and those who don't, they can walk on.

KC: By the way, this chapter is called "Dark Stars" and I know Jim gave you the title and it fits us, because of how Michael and I went out and we all know Jim certainly had a dark side.

Mic: Yes but, that is the point. We were at times, perhaps "dark stars" and the ending for both myself and Kurt Cobain was certainly not pleasant but we are not that now. The three of us hear speaking with you, have evolved. Jim is still in an amount of darkness not because he hasn't worked hard to evolve, he most certainly has, but he has to wait to be rejoined with his other half to really know the light I am now experiencing. I want to be clear though, Kurt

Cobain, Jim Morrison and myself (Michael Hutchence) may have had this darkness around us at times but it's no more. We are, essentially of the light and we have changed (for the better).

There are opportunities for each of you on earth to grow, learn, evolve and become more aligned with the truth, wisdom and the love that sometimes you choose to now push away. You can certainly do better on earth more than likely than you are doing now, but this side is a mere continuation and a new world where the possibilities are limitless.

Jim: We are no longer dark stars and don't want to be considered that. In fact, we don't want to be considered stars at all. It's not healthy to hold onto us as we were on earth. Can you please let us go? There are great philosophers for you to study and become fans of, great literature to absorb. It's not that we look down upon you for listening to our music but we don't think it's healthy of you to be fans of ours, or anyone else's.

KC: True, it's not a good thing to live in the past on earth. It's gone and earth life is about living in the present. I am always grateful people still listen to the music I left behind but that's as far it should go. The obsession over how I died, or how I lived is about pulling things out of a time capsule. Why not create your own time capsule and place the books, the music, the memories, and your own writings in it? Preserve it for those to come in the future so they can feel who you were. I say were, because you may not be the same over here and I am thankful I am not. My time capsule is the music, words and to some extent, the interviews I left behind. After you visited my capsule, why go further to see what others have to say about it? Shouldn't it be about what it means to you, not the next person? After you visit, go to something else.

Mic: Right, you know my former group reformulated and I am over the 20 years I spent with them. I can't live for that or dwell on it. I hope people liked or can find something in some of the music I have done, but beyond that, Jim, Kurt and I are giving their fans what they feel is of the utmost importance, there are great philosophers to study and so much more on earth than dead rock stars (Laughter from Kurt, Jim and Michael).

Jac: Ok well would anyone of you like to offer some suggestions of some interesting philosophers to study?

Jim: Well I am pretty sure, some of my fans like to discover the things they have heard about that I was into on earth but from here, I can offer some additional suggestions. The first one would be the writings of a great philosopher named Jiddu Krishnamurti. I am excited to share, I have met him on this side and he is a great teacher over here as he was on earth. I would suggest people study his teachings on breaking with the past, it will help them understand what we are trying to present here. His themes were what mine often were, fear and pleasure. I would suggest his work published called *"Krishnamurti's Notebook."* I think some of my fans will see much of what I tried to convey, in a much brighter light in his works. He kept notebooks as I did and his are a wealth of spiritual knowledge. I would ask any fan of mine to really tune into Jiddu Krishnamurti. I would also ask them to use their own guidance and find things to read that they are drawn to.

I would also suggest a study of the great philosopher, Sir Francis Bacon.
I contend the writings of Sir Francis are of great importance to all of you on the planet earth now.

I admire his discontent with Aristotle in *"Novum Organum"* and his use of deductive logic could not be more important at the time and place you are now in your history.

One of the most important books that influenced me subconsciously much more so than I ever realized is called, *"The New Atlantis"* and thankfully published about a year after Sir Francis ascended to this side. Why do I believe the *"The New Atlantis"* is so important? Very simply put, it signifies the true search for natural philosophy, which has been obscured for way too long. It's a much more complicated work than most realize and one of the most brilliant books I contend ever written. *"The New Atlantis"* is not simply a novel about how science and religion intersect; in truth, it has many levels as does the think tank, Solomon's House. It's quite Machiavellian and full of the divinely inspired wisdom of ancient adepts as it is quite encrypted in its meanings. Was it the model for America? Only you can decide!

Mic: Very good choices. I would urge anyone who has never read *"The Picture of Dorian Gray"* by Oscar Wilde to dive right in. There is so much to this book about being on earth even in the times you now live, you will be amazed. I would also encourage any of the works by Timothy Freke, pertaining to Christianity but of course, there is much to explore in terms of Buddhism and Taoism. I would suggest you study as many branches of spirituality as you can and find the right one for you. I urge a study of the Kabbalah for any and everyone as well. You will at the very least, gather concepts from these different branches and be able to create your own, unique tree that blossoms and grows for many years to come.

KC: I would suggest William S. Burroughs for my fans. I read him on earth and he is really exceptional. I guess you could say and different and I think my fans would get a lot out of him. I think musically, I was a fan of lots of alternative stuff but you know now, I would tell my fans to check out Ani De Franco. Her lyrics are pretty amazing to me. She is a real artist. I would also suggest you keep journals or diaries. Write it all down and put your thoughts on paper. Preserve your soul.

Jim: I think it's time to put this to bed now Jacquie.

Jac: It's been a wonderful experience and I am really grateful for it.

Mic: Same for us, we are grateful for you and you are indeed the teacher we wait for in our soul group. Your knowledge is immense on this side.

KC: And we are works in progress, can't wait 'til you're here holding class.

Mic: I think to sum this up, we wanted to share some of what we have learned and where we are on this side but we also wanted to ask our fans to let us go.

KC: Obsession never served anyone well, it becomes addiction that kills all there is. Please save your tears for me, Jim and Michael. We thank you for being so interested but we want you to go on and spend your time on earth on more enlightening things.

Jim: Yes please don't follow us anymore. Let us go, let us be. We came through to this one channel. None of us have plans to go to any other.

Mic: This is true but for the fact if someone we really want to communicate with is in front of a gifted medium, we would certainly try and come through clearly.

KC: Precisely, but not to channel to anyone anymore. So having said that, we will exit now, we were dark stars, we are happy to say, we are brighter now, lighter now and happier among the true stars (those of the sky), than we ever were on earth.

Mic: With great affection, I bid you adieu.

Jim: As we leave you, we hope you finally realize, there was more to us than what those on earth claim, and we are not the same. We are better now than we ever were, but I won't be me, not entirely, until I am with her.

Made in the USA
Lexington, KY
08 May 2015